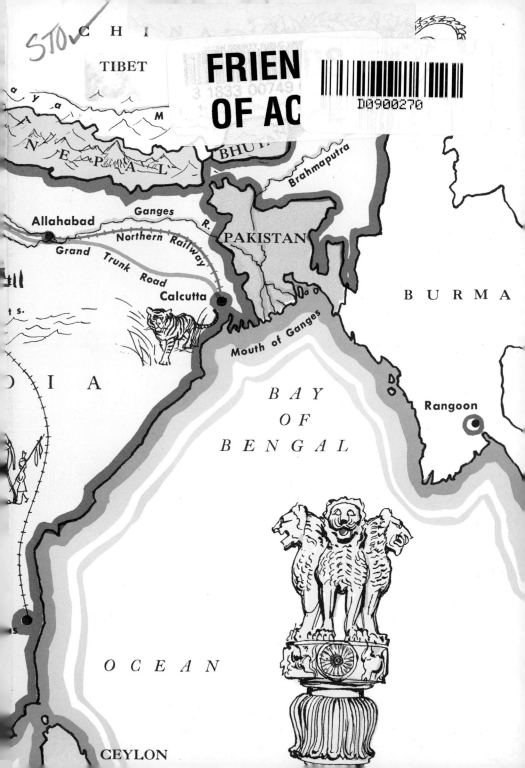

CHINA

TIBET

a
y
a
M

NEPAL

BHUT

Brahmaputra

Allahabad

Ganges

R.

PAKISTAN

Northern Railway

Grand Trunk Road

Calcutta

BURMA

Mouth of Ganges

t s.

DIA

Rangoon

BAY

OF

BENGAL

OCEAN

CEYLON

DELHI
OLD & NEW

An arched street in Old Delhi

DELHI
OLD
& NEW

By **EMILY POLK**
Illustrated by **EMIL WEISS**

RAND McNALLY & COMPANY
Chicago   New York   San Francisco

THE CITIES OF THE WORLD SERIES
(*Already Published*)

Paris by Irene Smith, illustrated by Emil Weiss
San Francisco by Jean Fritz, illustrated by Emil Weiss
London by Maurice Rosenbaum, illustrated by Rosemary
  Aldridge

SPELLING AND PRONUNCIATION

Hindi, the language of North India and official language of the whole nation, has a different alphabet from English, just as Russian, Greek, and others do. These languages are rewritten in our alphabet by a process known as transliteration. No spelling in another alphabet is exact, nor can it be considered the only "right" spelling. This book uses the official Government of India spelling for the Indian proper names and for names of places and monuments, without attempting to give the approximate English pronunciation. But it is important to know the correct pronunciation of the capital city: Delhi is pronounced *Dell*-lee.

CONTENTS

ILLUSTRATIONS

SUGGESTED DRIVES

I.

A CITY WITH NINE LIVES

Spread like an Oriental carpet on the brown north-
ern plains, New Delhi, India's great capital city, glows in
the sun. Air travelers, pressing against the windows, look
down—red-stone buildings, green trees, the flash of fountains, a silver river. The plane banks north: below are
domes, minarets, crowded bazaars—it is Old Delhi. East,
and below, the Yamuna River curves past the city. Circling south, over the hollow ruins of massive citadels, the
plane slides down west to land at Palam, the International
Airport.

A clamor of greetings and good-bys in Hindi and a
dozen other languages fills the air. Bright with the colored
saris and jewels of Indian women, the airport lounge is
as gay as a festival of nations. Dark-eyed children run to
see the planes. Tourists stream in, and men of science and
of business, writers, photographers, artists, dreamers, and
diplomats. Special visitors, wearing garlands of flowers,
shake hands with delegations. Cameras click. The whole
world has turned its eyes on this vivid land.

Now a turbaned porter puts the luggage into a car

and the bustling scene is left behind. Ready for fresh adventures, the new arrivals speed through a flat rolling prairie dotted with trees, little tombs, and temples. Here is the timeless horizon of India . . . and suddenly they are in Delhi, a city that is two cities, one called Old, one named New, a Phoenix city, rich with the exciting wonders of a nation that is modern and ancient—a nation of many ages rolled into one.

Today most people come by air. But racing side by side, from the Bay of Bengal nine hundred miles east, across green rice fields and the fertile valley of the Ganges, historic Grand Trunk Road, and the Northern Railway link Calcutta to the capital. From Madras, thirteen hundred miles south, the trains come whistling past farms and thatched villages; wooded glades echo as engines labor through the Vindhya Hills. And a road and railway, swinging inland from Bombay, the western seaport city, follow an eight-hundred-mile pilgrim route laid along these brown hills and millet fields two thousand years ago.

Every November thousands of sightseers leave the cold of Europe and America to troop around monuments and blue-tiled tombs in the Indian sunshine. All winter they come. They finger silks and delicate woolens; sample rich, spicy curries. On the sidewalk near their modern hotel they buy old brass and copper objects of art, or watch an age-old sight of story-book fame—glittering serpents swaying to the reed-flute music of a ragged snake charmer. They motor off to ride elephants at Jaipur and to see the marble Taj Mahal at Agra gleam white in the moonlight. Until the April sun begins to burn they pour

10

Brass and copper objects of art

through Delhi's museums and galleries marveling at the unique arts of India.

Above New Delhi's roof of trees, the sky is bright with sunlight. Even in winter it drenches the air and dazzles the eye. But streets are leafy tunnels, and visitors driving down them feel the fascination of the city's regal beauty. Low, white-columned houses are poised with graceful elegance on acres of shaded lawns. Deep shadows accent the massive dignity of the public buildings. Princely palaces, highlighted by the sun, stand in green parks, and everywhere is an atmosphere of space and calm. Parkways border the tree-crowned avenues; here there are no sidewalks, no idling crowds. Now and then little yellow taxis tear frantically along, limousines swish past, a brace of bicycles, and a motorscooter dodge away. Visitors are charmed by this air of suburban tranquillity.

But soon they come to Connaught Place, the handsome business and shopping circle of New Delhi. The tempo steps up. Automobiles and motorcycles whirl around the central circular park of fountains and trees past the white columns of the continuous arcade. Strolling in its shade, tourists and townspeople look into windows richly hung with silks and filled with a thousand treasures. The fashionable cafés, air-conditioned, are packed with customers slowly sipping morning iced coffee or, afternoons, cups of tea.

Briefly, at rush hour, pandemonium reigns here. All of the city's taxis, limousines, bicycles, and motorscooters seem to converge to tangle with waves of people surging from offices and shops. Brakes screech, horns blare; then suddenly they are gone. The splash of fountains can be heard again, trees and flowering bougainvillaea glow with sunset brilliance. Late shoppers wander into the shops

Connaught Place at rush hour

India Gate at night, with illuminated fountains

or promenade around the arcade to see who's in town.

Connaught Place is one of the pivot points for New Delhi streets. Straight south, down Curzon Road—an avenue of fine homes, Georgian buildings, and offices—is another focus of the radial street plan. It is the War Memorial Arch (popularly called India Gate), a great monumental arch of carved sandstone. From this memorial, the splendid mile-long Central Vista sweeps west, up row on row of terraces, fountains, esplanades, and carved walls to the crowning spectacle of the nation—its Capitol buildings, called the Secretariat and the President's House—

towering symbols of national dignity and grandeur. Of red and white sandstone, carved into turrets and domes of a rarely seen, beautiful style, they stand in isolation, serene above the city, on Raisina Hill. This is a suitable place for them, for Raisina Hill is a spur of the historically famous Ridge, northern part of the Aravalli Range, the oldest mountains in the world.

Travelers drive up Raisina Hill to see the panorama of New Delhi. But all of India seems to stretch endlessly out below. Pools shimmer on the Vista green, and the red stone of buildings, sharply defined in the clear, sunny air, glows like coral. Looking south, a distant tower beckons from ancient times. Looking in the opposite direction, toward Parliament Street, new buildings jut with white staccato emphasis from the sea of trees. And far beyond—just glimpsed from the Capitol buildings as a jumble of flat roofs, gilded domes, and slender minarets—is the exotic skyline of Old Delhi, the eighth city and capital of the Mogul Dynasty.

Alive with the high spirits of India, the Old City is home to most of Delhi's two millions. Every weekday morning, men stream out to work in all parts of the city. Those bound for the big offices and shops either cram into buses and careen off down miles of streets to New Delhi, or jump on bicycles and whir away, tens of thousands strong.

But many stay right where they are. From shops just big enough to sit in, they sell hardware, shoes, cloth, trinkets, things to eat, and almost any object imaginable. Rare antiques have come from these little shops. And all

14

day men rush up and down, and sometimes right into the street traffic, carrying head baskets or pushing handcarts, to add their bit to a tangle of horse carts, bullock carts, bicycles, trucks, and decrepit cars. Occasionally a farmer rides a camel into town, bags of grain for the market slung on each side. The great beast wades into the thick of it, with his bored expression unchanged.

But it is the people who make these bazaars uproarious and colorful. With high good humor they bargain, gossip, and laugh, walk, run, and sit along the sidewalks and in the streets. They love crowding together when they are not busy, to talk or play cards under a big tree, or in a shaded doorway. And forever underfoot are little boys engrossed in hopscotch, knuckle-bone, or football.

The most famous buildings of Old Delhi are the Friday Mosque and a Mogul citadel called the Red Fort, from the color of its stone. Life in the Old City centers on a

Children, sitting in doorways, in Old Delhi

15

Caparisoned elephant with swaying howdah

wide street that issues from the west gate of the Red Fort. This is Chandni Chowk—Street of Moonlight—and although it is now the noisiest and busiest bazaar of all, it was originally laid out in the grand manner, with trees and a canal, to be the thoroughfare for royal processions. For two hundred years caparisoned elephants paraded down it with sultans, queens, and princely children in the swaying gilt and silk-cushioned howdahs. The people cheered from the balconies that still line each side of the street. After the British conquered India, that world vanished, never to reappear.

Although crowded to saturation point, there are in Old Delhi a few quiet lanes where old palaces—carved doors and blue tiles intact—harbor a leisurely, graceful life left over from traditional India.

On the outskirts of the Old City mills and foundries

16

have sprung up. The sons of small shopkeepers and arti-
sans, lured by steady pay and better working conditions,
are leaving the family business, with its ups and downs, to
work in the mills. The age-old crafts—jewelry making,
ivory and wood carving, leather work, and gold embroi-
dering—still compete for young hands. But how long can
they carry on? The pace of industrialization is fast in
India.

Old Delhi is one of the nation's most famous jewelry
centers. But the jewelry bazaar is a shabby maze of dim,
arcaded narrow lanes lined by dilapidated buildings hidden from view by the arcade roof. Here are one-room
shops and factories where a family will have lived and
worked for generations. Every corner has its occupant.
In a small street-front shop, sitting cross-legged on a white
mat, a man is busy selling jewelry. In another tiny room,
just behind, his brother is busy making it. A forge glows,
a small hammer tinkles against the gold or silver. Some-

*A small hammer tinkles as the
silversmith makes his jewelry*

17

where in the building above, their families are preparing the big three-o'clock meal of the day.

Next door to them may be another jeweler, a cloth merchant, or a turbaned tailor pedaling his old sewing machine with hard, bare feet; or even a little restaurant with a chair or two, a table, a stove and an all-pervading, delicious smell of savory, spiced, and pepper-hot foods.

In the street, hawkers trudge on the worn stones, baskets heaped with fruits or vegetables on their heads. From earliest morning their cries, mingling with motor horns, shouts of bullock drivers, and the harsh caw of crows, produce the background effects of the Oriental bazaar.

Everything that an Indian family wants comes past the door. The barber with his bowl and scissors steps in to trim father's and brother's hair. The sari salesman brings his box of silk or cotton saris for the women of the family to choose from. Wicker chairs and cooking pots come past, tied to bicycles or carried in head baskets. But the most popular hawker is the *paan* man. From his tray of little dishes he makes on the spot this Indian favorite—a mixture of scented powders and pieces of betel nut wrapped in a bright-green, tongue-tingling leaf. It can be chewed for hours and is the Indian version of chewing gum. The window ledge heaped with brown, homemade cigarettes—the local tobacco shop—plays second best to the *paan* man.

During the days of the emperors, certain Old Delhi restaurants were famous for their choice Mogul delicacies. Connoisseurs of exotic foods traveled long distances to dine there. Only a few serve true Mogul specialties now. In these small, shadowy rooms every current of air carries the fragrances of Oriental cooking, of spices and broiling meats and hot butter. With everything cooked to order, and expensive, most people cannot now spare the time or money to patronize these restaurants.

But often you will see sleek automobiles gleaming in the light of a big sign on an old building where a plain little restaurant serves delicious Punjab specialties of Tandoori cooking. Whole chickens or fresh river fish, sauced with paprika, spices, and sour cream, and impaled on long spears, are held over glowing charcoal, in enormous clay pots (the tandoors). Eaten with the fingers, hot off the spear, these foods are immensely popular with everyone. An unforgettable scene at night is a dim, fire-lit room where the staff of perspiring, flame-reddened cooks lean with their spears over the great red pots.

Food served here, on in any big hotel or restaurant, is especially prepared for visitors to India. In trains or bazaars, freshly cooked, fire-hot food is safe to eat, but not cold food or overripe fruits, or fruits with broken skins.

Disguised by unfamiliar names, most foods are, in fact, familiar. Exceptions are water-lily bulbs sliced into thin perforated rings, deep-fried and crunchy as potato chips; a terrifying spinach—fortunately, seldom come across— tasting like essence of blue vitriol; three kinds of hot, green chili-peppers—those that merely burn your mouth, those that slightly stun you, and those that knock you out.

At the sprawling, red-brick railway station in Old

*A dim, fire-lit room, where the staff of flame-reddened
cooks lean with their spears over the great tandoors*

Delhi a scene of nightmare confusion develops when the trains from all over India roll in. Everyone runs, suitcases spill, but tempers stay level, for traveling by train is a favorite national pastime. Indians, with their natural exuberance, love the excitement of trains. The Public Library and the Municipal Offices are in the station vicinity. In this congested area—and as the city becomes more and more crowded, shops and shacks try to fill every vacant nook—the most cluttered square will be adorned with a beautiful small mosque in a quiet courtyard. It is an intriguing part of town, not often seen by foreign travelers.

North, through Kashmiri Gate, beyond Old Delhi's tumultuous life, the road curves along parks and grassy fields and past walled gardens. This is the Civil Lines where the British lived until 1930 when New Delhi was completed. Some of their old mansions are now the headquarters of the Police and Foreign Registration Offices. The old Vice-Regal Lodge—as the British governor's mansion was called—houses Delhi University. Its extensive grounds make a wonderful campus for over ten thousand local students and some three thousand from other parts of India and the world. A famous private school for boys, St. Stephens, is in the Civil Lines.

The best schools for girls, and most of the primary schools, are in New Delhi. But India needs many more schools and is making efforts to have them. Boys and girls not enrolled in schools are taught at home by tutors or by their parents. At the end of the term they take school examinations like the other children. Most of the modern schools were started by the British, but some

21

—missionary and other kinds—are run like American schools.

The very few Indian boys and girls whose fathers are in the Diplomatic Service, or head a big industry or business, live much like Western young people. Out of school there is swimming and tennis at the clubs, picnics, and horseback riding. As in other British-influenced countries, cricket is India's most popular sport, followed by football and hockey. At "coke" time, teenagers crowd their favorite restaurants at Connaught Place and try out the newest Hollywood dance, seen in the latest movie.

But the vast majority of Indians and their children live a closely knit family life. The joint family system is an ancient and strong tradition. As many as eighty members of a family may live together in one large house, and there are always plenty of cousins for companionship. In

Cricket is India's most popular sport

poor families, everyone works. Even the smallest children follow their parents around, learning what their duties will be as they grow older. This leaves them very little time for play.

Like the medieval cities of Europe, Delhi had its Great Wall and City Gates circled by a moat and road. The city, on its way to becoming a modern metropolis, outgrew them long ago. But as it grew, the old plan shaped it, creating its special character. Just as Kashmiri Gate and Ajmeri Gate pointed the ancient ways to Kashmir and Ajmer, the tall gate arches still stand, bestowing their proud names on the new streets and districts. Boulevards in ever widening circles sweep around them and past a few picturesque fragments of the vanished wall. Fortunately, the city's planners have enshrined even small ruins in little parks and garden enclosures; the people of Delhi are aware of their rich inheritance. There's a charm in the surprise of suddenly seeing a tumbled bit of dark vine-covered wall on a modern street.

The city's history could be read in street names. Romantic Mogul names and names of British viceroys and generals are prominent both in Old and New Delhi. The British Minto, Curzon, and Irwin, the Great Moguls Akbar, Aurangzeb, and Shah Jahan are some of India's men of destiny who are honored in this way. Traveling Americans are surprised to find Indian and American history touching in a street named for one British Governor-General, Lord Cornwallis, who came to India soon after his defeat in America.

About four hundred public buses, rushing between

the Old and New Cities, carry three hundred thousand citizens a day. Rattling streetcars, that are none too tidy, shuttle along at three miles an hour with their quota of the rush-hour crowd. But the main way of travel between work and home is by bicycle. At the peak of the rush hour they are an awe-inspiring sight—some two hundred thousand of them, pedaled ten abreast down the main street, oblivious of the traffic havoc they create.

The customs of this ancient land have largely given way to modern demands. Big offices open at nine and close at five, with a scant hour for lunch—but not in the depths of the Old City. There merchants keep the old ways. They slide languidly onto their white cushions at ten o'clock and lock up again at three to eat and then rest through the highest heat of the day. From seven until ten at night, every shop is wide open and the bazaar is

Pottery market

busy. These are tropical hours regulated by the thermometer instead of the clock.

Indian people like the evening and early morning best. In the evening, family groups stroll through brightly-lit streets awash with a dissonant din of lively songs pouring at full volume from shop radios. A sweets vendor busily dips pastry balls from syrup with his long-handled spoon for shoppers to eat as they meander along. In winter the strollers are wrapped in warm woolen shawls; in summer the thinnest possible cotton, and on very hot evenings some men and boys go bare-chested. Indians are sociable people and laughter loving. The evening bazaars are like a great party. Strangers talk freely together, with everyone in the immediate neighborhood joining in. The favorite Indian pastime is visiting friends.

Almost everyone gets up at dawn, so as not to miss

a minute of fresh cool air. But in contrast to gossipy evenings, mornings are quiet; it is the customary time for prayers and meditation. From some high, distant minaret, a sheer, arching cry lifts calmly again and again over the dark, sleeping city—the *muezzin* is calling Delhi's Muslims to their dawn prayers. Most homes have a small shrine, or prayer room—the humblest have a small prayer corner—and each member of the family, bathed and in clean white clothes, performs his prayer ritual. Then he may go out to walk quietly in an open space—a balcony, or roof deck, or garden, or perhaps in one of the city parks.

The muezzin calls Delhi's Muslims to their dawn prayers

New Delhi is a garden city all year. Avenues are lined with trees that never lose their leaves. Anyone familiar with New Delhi can tell by the trees what street he is on, because each street is planted with a different kind—tamarind, neem, peepul, and other stately deciduous Indian varieties. Thick-crowned, they turn back the fierce summer sun, and in the cool shadow gathered under them, weary people rest on the ground and forget the heat for a moment.

In late spring the magnificent flowering trees flaunt their colors, painting the city with the brilliant splashes of scarlet Gul Mohur, yellow laburnum, purple jacaranda and pink acacia. Everyone turns out to stride through the public parks; hearts are lifted by this yearly celebration of the trees. The air glows when the sun strikes the flowers. Dropping petals dye a circle of pure color on the ground.

Many New Delhi homes of high government officials stand in four or five landscaped acres. Most homes have some sort of grass and flower plot. Even crowded neighborhoods have parks nearby. Climate and traditions of work and play make it a city whose people like to spend the days indoors, dawns and evenings in gardens. With their long months of near-inferno weather (in May and June the temperature can reach 105°), Indians take special delight in silvery dew-drenched morning lawns, or an evening walk on cool grass after a hot day.

Out on the Central Vista—this greensward of over six hundred acres cools the air quickly after sundown— thousands of people sit on the grass every summer evening. On one of the ornamental lakes families can rent small boats and row among the water lilies. As dark falls they put on thin wraps, for by contrast with the day, night seems chilly. Lights play on the arching fountain waters, and overhead the clear, black sky is diamond-studded.

Within a few miles in any direction from India Gate are hundreds of acres reserved as recreation areas. Each of the major tombs—the Lodi Kings'; Prince Safdar Jung's; Humayun's, second King of the Mogul Dynasty— stands in a park of trees and shrubs traced with winding paths. Near Purana Qila, remnant of the fortress built by Sher Shah over the prehistoric first city, Indra Prasthna, is the ever-popular New Delhi Zoo. Here the animals roam about in cleverly concealed enclosures as if free in their natural surroundings. And deep in a vast semi-wild tract of wooded ravines, just across the highway from the foreign embassies, are the romantic ruins of Emperor Aurangzeb's Hunting Lodge. Sometimes picnickers, lounging on the roof until late afternoon, see wild peacocks strut and dance under the jungle acacia trees.

India is a democratic republic with a parliament like England's. The world's biggest free elections are held throughout the twenty-five states and territories every five years. Greater Delhi, like Washington D.C., is governed not as a state, but as a small Union Territory. The National Government appoints a Commissioner, an Ad-

One of the Lodi tombs

28

Animals roam about as if in their natural surroundings

visory Council, and two Advisory Boards to help him
with administration, industrial problems, and public rela-
tions.

Delhi Territory includes New Delhi, Delhi (popularly called Old Delhi), and the adjacent countryside of
truck gardens, old villages, and model-village projects. It
covers over four hundred square miles; one hundred sev-
enty square miles of it are taken up by the two cities.
New Delhi has its Municipal Committee headed by a
President, and Old Delhi has a corporation of eight
elected members who in turn elect a Mayor and Deputy
Mayor. They all work for efficient city government, but
the President of spacious New Delhi, where, in some
areas, there are only three families to an acre, must have
an easier time than the Mayor of Old Delhi, where people
are crammed a thousand to the acre.

*Athletic policemen stand
out of harm's way*

At the intersections of both cities, athletic policemen, unarmed but for a small club, pivot all day, directing the headlong tangle of vehicles. They stand out of harm's way on concrete platforms under big white umbrellas. With red fringe swinging from jaunty turbans, their smart khaki shorts and shirts, handsome, but stern and rather haughty, faces, and muscular grace give them the necessary authority for almost any situation.

During the lavish days of the Moguls, Delhi—our Old Delhi—housed some hundred thousand people. A hundred and fifty years ago when the British marched up from Bengal and, routing the army of the Maharaja of Sindia, captured Delhi, the population was about the same. It started to grow when the British moved the capital from Calcutta in 1911. They did this for several reasons, principally historical and administrative. But they also preferred the crisp winter climate and dry air to the humidity of Calcutta. And, too, the Himalaya Mountains are only a few hours' drive away. This "Roof of the World" has breathtaking scenery—snow-capped peaks soar above lakes; there are forested valleys, splashing cascades, and range after range of glorious mountains.

India became an independent nation on August 15, 1947. Suddenly, from the area that became Pakistan, uprooted people swept in. The city's population jumped in less than a month from a few hundred thousand to almost a million and a half. Housing colonies were thrown together to shelter them. Thousands of new businesses, factories, and shops developed within a year to give them work.

It was one evening, during the turmoil of those first months, in a New Delhi garden filled with the peace of trees and flowers, that Mahatma Gandhi was killed by a

Rajghat, Gandhi's shrine near Old Delhi

fanatic's bullet. Gandhi, India's great man of peace, had led his people to this independent nationhood. His last words, "Hei Ram," a cry to his God, are engraved on his shrine at Rajghat near Old Delhi.

The city continues to grow. As Greater Delhi, it spreads out, absorbing villages and farms in the usual metropolitan manner. Industries, attracted by a supply of workers, expand on the rim of the Old City. Residential suburbs spring up almost overnight on the monument-studded hills near New Delhi. The changes come so quickly that, on a return visit to a favorite picnic spot, one may find that bulldozers have cleared away its natural charms to make room for a factory or a housing development.

On these hills, ancient structures, inured to mere years, tell of other cities. Since the far-off heroic days of myth and legend, kings have built their capitals on the plains of Kuruk Shetra between the Aravalli Ridge and the sacred Yamuna River. The ruins of these eight other cities bring magic to Delhi's landscape. The march of history has strewn rich mementos around this bright modern capital city, New Delhi.

II.

BETWEEN RIDGE AND RIVER

The mighty Himalayas—greatest mountain range in the world—stretch across the entire top of India. These mountains (their name means "The Abode of Snow") have made India what it is—a land of tremendous drama and of extremes in everything. They turn back cold Siberian winds, shut in and build up the heat of the Equator's fiery sun. Each June, blue-black, water-filled clouds thunder up from the South Pole. Beating against this massive wall they pour out the furious monsoon rains. The Himalayas are India's climate-maker and first line of defense from northern invaders.

But the Indian mainland has a second line: two natural guardians protect its rich south-tapering peninsula—the Aravalli Ridge and the Yamuna River. The narrow gap between ridge and river, where Delhi stands, is the geographic and historic Gateway to India.

In an age so remote that only small pieces of pottery, brick, and dim folk memories remain, the first Gateway City was built. Called Indra Prasthna, it was the capital of a powerful Kuru tribe, the Pandavas. They were

An Aryan chariot

Aryans, cousins of the Celts and Teutons. Nomadic, war-like, they wandered south through eastern Europe with the cattle and horses they had tamed. A wild lot, tall and rangy with green eyes and red hair, fighters, hunters, horsemen, dashing charioteers full of restless, reckless courage, they worshiped elements that were like them-selves—Fire, Water, Thunder, the Lightning, and the Sun.

When snow melted in the Afghan passes, the Kurus filed through into India. They moved south, conquering the peaceful people they came across. At the Aravalli Range they turned east. Half-wooded, rolling land stretched before them. The young men rushed ahead out of sheer high spirits, flew back, horses frothing, to the slow procession of elders—priests and nobles and their king. Following the men were the women, girls, and small children. Except in times of danger, boys made a small procession near their fathers.

Behind, paced herds guarded by the clan's best horse-men. Cattle wealth meant a nomadic tribe's well-being; these hearty people lived principally on milk and meat.

An Aryan tribe's duties were divided among families. Some were custodians of ancient lore—the Brahmins. Their work was to remember and pass down the tribal teachings, to perform devotional rituals. The Kshatriyas protected the tribe: the hunters, cattle guards, warriors, and their chief. The Vaisyas carried forward the tribal business: barter, trade, and manufacture and, later, farming. The Sudhras served the other three groups. Conquered people were enslaved. Called Dasyus, they were outcasts—not part of the conqueror's social system. For thousands of years, until modern India made caste discriminations unlawful, every detail of life was governed by this system. But a person's aptitudes might determine his place in the division of work. The tribal Indian-Aryans mixed and ate together freely. At great camps they feasted, laughed, told heroic tales. Every dawn, priests chanted noble Aryan hymns that even today, when translated from the original Sanskrit, are very stirring. After several weeks of grazing the herds, they moved on.

The Aravalli Ridge lay low on the horizon to their right, a dark line striking up from the parched Southwest. Gradually it tapered off like an arm stretched out to clutch something. And just beyond its reach they found a great river. Here was everything their hearts could want: rich forests and grazing lands to the north and south, the ridge and river for their defensive, religious, and water needs.

Today one can peer into excavations and see tiny bricks that once made Indra Prasthna. The forests have gone, but this is the sacred ground—the legendary Plains of Kuruk Shetra, scene of a divine battle in that greatest of Indian epics, the Maha Bharata.

In the thirty-five hundred years since then, many invaders, fired by tales of fabulous wealth, poured through the northwest passages called the Hindu Kush. Cyrus, the Persian, in the sixth century B.C., sent his hordes into India. An audacious young Macedonian prince called Alexander the Great came in 327 B.C., and fought a succession of Hindu kings until his men rebelled. In three years of campaigns he did not reach the Yamuna. But others challenged these natural defenses and funneled through this strategic portal.

The Jade Route from China wound over the Himalayas past glacier and cataract, along cliff face and down valley, bringing merchants, scholars, and adventurers. They all came here; between ridge and river they entered the reality of India.

Kings and dynasties rose and fell, but about 400 A.D. a Punjab chieftain, King Dilleep, conquered Indra Prasthna. He renamed this first city Dilli Pur, christening for all time the succession of great capitals called Delhi. Overland traders from all the luxury-hungry world came to Delhi. Backed by fertile lands to the north, a trading center flourished. It drew up jewels and gold from the South, silks and brocades from the East through a sunburst of caravan roads that penetrated the length and breadth of India. Then, as now, Delhi, the focal point of all highways, stirred with high and often desperate adventure. Its strategic importance became a legend—"He who holds Delhi holds India."

Except for defense, the river played a secondary part in the life of the city. There was and is today little waterborne trade; a few small boats ply up and down with local produce.

The Yamuna can be temperamental. In spring, when the Himalayan snows melt, and especially after the monsoons, the river may rise with a rush. She pushes aside all restraints, sweeps away houses built too near. Over the centuries she has changed course many times. In spite of levees and artificial channels, parts of New Delhi may be knee-deep in flood water any October morning.

People escaping from homes too near the temperamental Yamuna River

This kicking-over-the-traces can be expected of a river that plunges down mountain ravines, a wild torrent raising an exultant roar as it rushes from the icy heights of Tibet toward the Indian plains. Released then from the demands of gravity, broadened and mellowed by a burden of tawny silt, it becomes a great river, and, to the nature-adoring Hindu people, a serene goddess—the auburn-haired Yamuna.

To Hindus, rivers have unique meaning, are loved and feared as if they were living goddesses. The ashes of Hindu dead are given to the river's care. On the banks of the Yamuna, at Delhi, are cremation terraces and a riverside temple. An atmosphere of strange beauty sometimes fills these religious places. The small white temple stands under a tree so old that it leans almost longingly toward the water. Stone steps, wide as terraces, go down the

Cremation terraces on the banks of the Yamuna,

bank; the river laps over the bottom steps. At dawn, sunset, and other hours, the temple priests chant their prayers. A bell-like tone rings out in quick delicate rhythm from little hand-held cymbals. Silvery echoes float over the silently moving amber water.

Traditionally, only one bank of Indian rivers is built upon. It is the holy side; the other, left wild, is thought to be ill-omened. India's picturesque cities and towns, with their trees, prayer-steps, and temples, are usually found on the right bank of the down-current. Such fears are giving way to modern needs and, at Delhi, outside the city, water-using industries are on both sides of the Yamuna. For most of its length, small country craft are poled slowly along. There is a margin of sandy bank, near which river terns fly low, hunting white-fleshed rohee, the delectable river fish.

with white riverside temple and broad stone steps

Divine protectress and ancient friend, the river and the ridge brought up this city between them, gave it its first stir of life and its deepest meaning, shaped and educated it in the ways of the world.

An imaginary early-morning trip just south of New Delhi will conjure up the high drama of Delhi's youth.

Dawn comes late on Delhi winter mornings. At six, the stars are burning brightly in the dark sky. Beyond deserted streets with street lamps silvering the underside of trees, the highway unrolls swiftly through the dark, ahead of the car lights. Now and then, on both sides, the blackness thickens into great hunched shapes looming against the thin black of the sky—shadows of tombs of forgotten kings. A whisper of light spans the heavens, the smallest stars fade out. As the car turns east onto a side road, a sparkling jewel fairly leaps in the gray, high over the horizon. The morning star is saluting the sun.

Now, between night and day, the low, bare hills are dark, billowing shadows. The car pulls over to the side and stops. Not far away, on a slope, a few goats graze, watched by some sleepy boys—little ghosts wrapped from head to foot in white shawls, against the chill. One offers to guard the car. Another knows the trail and is hired as guide. A stiff, rocky climb—hurriedly, for the sun is almost up—and there on the broad hill, mammoth granite slabs, laid close together, form a great amphitheater.

Row below row of stone terraces circle down to a lake of six acres of clear spring water over a hundred feet deep. Water birds float on its surface. The sky glows

*A few goats graze on a slope, watched by sleepy boys
wrapped in white shawls*

pink. From the west bank, where a towering Temple of the Sun once stood, the water mirrors a glowing, reddening sky. And now in the east a point of vibrant red swells rapidly into a pure red sun. With a cry and rush of wings, the water birds soar up. . . . They are the last sun worshippers at Suraj Kund, Lake of the Sun, built by Anangpala of Delhi in the eleventh century as part of his capital city, Anangpur, second city of Delhi.

What scenes this water theater has held! The wide tiers circling, glittering, bejeweled, flower-draped; music, and royal parties feasting, laughing in the moonlight. Or, at dawn, hymns echoing from terrace to terrace, white-robed priests, gongs, cymbals, seashell trumpets, incense. At night, in shafts, in the lowest course of stones, torches were thrust and the lake flamed with a circle of reflected fire.

Modern daylight dissolves these phantoms. A path

Suraj Kund, Lake of the Sun

leads down the far side of the hill and over the gravel of an old watercourse. Beyond, a stream flows under branches of huge peepul trees that can live two thousand years. Suddenly looming above the trees, a dark vine-draped barrier, Anangpala's dam, blocks the ravine. Fifty feet high, its stones—some six feet square—are immense granite cubes cut from the Aravalli Ridge. Not a crack shows between them. High in the wall are several openings—spillways for the water once stored behind it. But in a thousand years the creek has quietly washed a small passage in the cliff and left its giant, would-be captor standing with empty hands.

This is a pleasant place to rest. A white cloth is spread on the grass and a second breakfast emerges from a basket packed by the hotel—cheese, fruit, a thermos jug of coffee. Some is offered to the little guide, but he looks shyly away—this is not his kind of food. Later, in a village hut, he'll dive into thin, roasted wheat cakes and a curried meat stew so red-pepper hot that tears come into his eyes.

The sun is well up, and sunlight dapples the leaves and stones. Pages of history seem to be opening all around. The brook murmurs to itself. Does it sing the famous folk ballad of King Prithviraj Chauhan, twelfth-century hero and chief of the proud Rajput clan? The romantic love story of this prince changed the history of India.

During his rule of the Delhi Kingdom, the second capital city, Anangpur, was renamed Rai Pithora. He extended it, beautified it with temples and gardens, and strengthened its walls, fearing the Turks who, greedy for the fabled "wealth of Ind," were harassing the frontiers.

43

And he enraged the powerful king of Kannauj by carrying off his favorite and most beautiful daughter, the high-spirited Sunjucta. Prithviraj built palaces for her and a tower so she could see the Yamuna.

But two thousand years of Indian isolation were about to end. In 1191, Prithviraj and his Rajput army of two hundred thousand horsemen and three thousand fighting elephants valiantly repulsed a horde of invaders. Within a year the Turks rallied, with greater numbers, and marched again. Now this ill-starred romance sparked flames of tragedy. In bitter revenge, Kannauj refused to send his army to help; it would have turned the tide. The Rajputs advanced against overwhelming forces and were defeated. Prithviraj, taken prisoner, was coldly put to the sword. And Sunjucta, some say, jumped to her death from her tower at Rai Pithora. The Turks swept on. In 1194 they took Kannauj and the king paid with his life for his treachery.

At Suraj Kund, the royal lovers may have watched the sunrise that fateful day of certain defeat. But a mystery is told on desert nights when Rajputs gather to sing their proud ballads. Who were those assassins that, leaping down a narrow pass, stabbed and killed the Turkish sultan, twelve years to the day after the defeat of Prithviraj? Surely Prithviraj was not dead but only blinded, wandering, training his men for final vengeance—this gallant last Hindu king of Delhi.

Returning from Suraj Kund, the car speeds down the tree-shaded highway. Suddenly a family of monkeys dashes across the road—five big ones and a baby clinging desperately to its mother's back. Ignoring the car, they lope along, then bound up a tree. We again speed west.

An impressive red-stone tower lifts its crown above the bare hills. It is the Qutb Minar of Rai Pithora. Some historians believe that it was built up from Sunjucta's tower. Over the centuries her tragic spirit may have impelled the many who leaped from it to their deaths. Today, to prevent these tragedies, the law requires that there must be at least three people in a climbing party.

A driveway leads through broad lawns to a promenade. Beyond stands the tall minar and the Qutb Mosque. This is the threshold to almost eight hundred years of stirring history. It began on a spring day in 1193 when the Great Slave, Qutb-ud-Din Aibak, strode here to take command of Rai Pithora. Huge, ugly, with ruthless

Closeup of Qutb Minar, showing details of carvings

45

Qutb Mosque, first Muslim house of worship in India

drive and keen intelligence, this Turk muscled through life from child-slave to Sultan of Delhi and the founding of the powerful Slave Dynasty. His first act as conqueror was to command that masons tear down all twenty-seven of their beautiful Hindu temples and build a mosque with the carved stones. Watching them, he planned a great minaret to proclaim his triumph. Soon his military campaigns brought splendor and prosperity to the capital. He made Delhi the nerve center of India.

How amazed Qutb-ud-Din would be to see today's stream of holidaying people from countries unheard of then. They stand, with heads stretched back, admiring the patterns on his triumphal tower; then wander in pavilions, through delicate, filtered gloom. Shadows, cool as evening, gathered under lofty domes, rest their sun-tired eyes. They mill around the carved Hindu columns of Qutb's Mosque, first Muslim house of worship in India. Qutb called it Quwwat-ul-Islam—the Might of Islam—as if prophesying the Indian future of his faith.

Built on the very heart of Prithviraj's citadel, the mosque is centered around a famous Iron Pillar. Anangpala is said to have brought it from eastern India to adorn his capital. Modern scientists, steel makers, and historians are amazed at this remarkable column. It is a solid shaft, over twenty-three feet high, of iron so pure that, after

Qutb Minar

The mosque is centered around a famous Iron Pillar

fifteen hundred years of monsoons, no rust has dimmed the smooth surface or dulled the crisp edge of its inscriptions. This is a feat of forging that modern men could not equal until the late nineteenth century. It tells much about the unrecorded epochs of Indian history; explains the fame, even in 300 B.C., of India's Kalinga steel, a tempered blue steel for swords, coveted by the kings of the ancient world.

But now it is time for us to climb the tower. We leave the bright sunlight to enter a small door on the north. A stairway swings up, taking us to successive heights of history through the darkness above. The only light and air come from slits at each half turn of the spiral. Twisting up, inside of the gradual taper, from a forty-six-foot diameter base, the steps are steep. Footsteps rasp in the dim shaft. Up and up the majestic Turkish sultans of Delhi have climbed before us.

First the Great Slave, Qutb, toiled up the 165 steps to this first balcony, then the broad top of his tower. In 1199 he laid the foundations and eventually built it up to this point, 90 feet in the air. Completed by others, it would become one of the world's most remarkable monuments. We can imagine his intense ugly face, the flash of his black eyes as he exults, looking out from the height at the panorama that marks his growing power. We look down at the remaining great arches of his mosque. Lightning-like letters of Arab script, carved on the first tower, salute him: "Amir of Amirs, Commander in Chief, Chief of the State, the Glorious, the Great . . ."

Another 90 steps, another balcony—the wide Delhi plains opening out; and again up 60 steps to the third level. It's rather frightening on this narrow ledge 185 feet from the ground. But the Government of India is very careful of its grandest tower. It is checked carefully and is safe; the stone railing is strong.

Iltamish, second Slave King, built these two sections of the minar. In 1220 they were completed. He climbed up to survey his kingdom and, being a deeply religious man, gave thanks to Allah. Iltamish was remarkably handsome. Standing on this high pinnacle, surrounded by his gorgeously dressed courtiers, he outshone them all with a natural majesty. His jeweled, plumed turban and tunic of gold brocade gleamed in the sun. He had indeed come far from the events of his childhood, when he was sold into slavery by brothers jealous of his striking looks and high intelligence. Not only did he bring the minar to this height, but also extended all of Qutb's other ambitions for the glory of Delhi.

From this third balcony, a dark geometry of trees and old walls shows us the pattern of the Imperial Delhi Iltamish saw. On the hills beyond we make out a tumbling granite mass. It is the oldest tomb in India, a fortress tomb called Ghori Durgah, built by Iltamish for his beloved eldest son, Prince Nazir. Indian sculptors, working in marble, fashioned an interior of white columns almost Greek in classic sorrow of form. Seen from the tower, it fades into the hills, a gray ghost of the monarch's grief for his son.

Our eyes are now adjusted to the hard noon light, to the monotone of low hills, the deceptive sweeping distances. Traces of buildings seem to rise from the ground on all sides. Some are rubble of battlements once surrounding the fortress of Rai Pithora. Near us on the northwest is an elaborate red sandstone tomb. It covers the grave of the great Iltamish. His daughter, fabulous Empress Reziya, Delhi's only queen, built it for him.

Young, capable, an energetic ruler, and very beautiful, Reziya even had a talent for war. Dressed in kingly tunic and turban, she rode fearlessly into battle at the head of her army. But Turkish princes would not bow to a woman. After four tempestuous years she was tricked into battle, deserted by her men, and murdered. A crumbling, unmarked grave in Old Delhi is said to be hers, proof of the nobles' scorn for a woman who dared to play king.

The heap of coarse stones below us to the south was

once a magnificent tomb. It is the House of Balban—Balban, last Slave Emperor of Delhi. How mightily he strode this third platform we stand so timidly on. His life story staggers the imagination. As a child in Turkey he was captured by savage Mongols. They sold him to a Moslem priest, who educated him and brought him to India. He was then bought by the sultan and became one of a famous band of men—the Forty Slaves of Iltamish. By sheer merit, strength of mind, and purpose he rose to the top. After Iltamish died, Balban's daughter married the young, frail Sultan Mahmud. Mahmud suddenly died. Balban stepped to the throne. Iron monarch, magnificent man, superb in his unbending dignity, for twenty-two momentous years, Balban exercised absolute, limitless power. He lived a regal, but austere life. His tomb, battered, unsightly now, was, in 1280, as imposing as Balban himself, Delhi's last Slave Sultan.

Around to the west we see, in the near distance, a little cluster of houses edging a pond. It is Mehrauli, a picturesque village settled among still elegant tombs and pavilions of the Slave Kings. Tourists visit it for a glimpse of the splendors lavished by those sultans on their capital. The ornate pavilion at water's edge then centered a fifty-acre lake entirely lined with red sandstone.

The centuries roll by, but each November, villagers in their red and yellow costumes have come to Mehrauli from miles around to celebrate a gay carnival begun in Slave-Sultan days, the Festival of the Flowers. Village music, wild gypsy music of the Punjab—original home of gypsies—throbs day and night. Young men leap and whirl

Young gypsy men leap and whirl

with wonderful abandon as dark-eyed girls watch the timeless country dances.

India is replete with festivals—countless ancient religious festivals with impressive and, to Western eyes, strange rituals. At the Brother Festival, sisters tie tinsel bracelets on their brothers' wrists, feed them favorite food, and sing to them, charmingly adopting as brothers-for-a-day those family friends without sisters.

The Color Festival is a popular multicolored bacchanal of powders and water sprays flung with wildest abandon on all who venture into the color-intoxicated crowds. Next day the roisterers return to their hard-working life, streaked with vivid reminders of the good time they had.

The Swing Festival is quaint and enchanting to watch. Every tree becomes a little circus of gaiety. It's a special day for little children, girls, and young women, all in their brightest clothes, swinging and singing. Pushing, flying through the air, or just dancing about, they cluster around the swing-tree from early morning until dusk.

The Brother Festival

Swinging is an ancient pastime in India. Sculptures of earliest times show large, ornately carved, slow-moving royal swings. The Moguls had beautiful ones inlaid and richly cushioned.

Delhi is a brighter place during the Spring Festival. Yellow is the color for spring. Everyone who can, wears brilliant yellow clothes. Even in Old Delhi, in the poorest, most crowded, parts, each person manages a little touch of the spring color. On the outskirts, and in villages, the excitement of spring inspires spirited dances. The drudgery of farming is all forgotten in a blaze of yellow. A bit

The Color Festival

The Alai Darwaza—Gatehouse of Alai

of dye transforms dull cotton, and girls in yellow saris, with yellow flowers braided into shining black hair, young men in yellow hip-cloths, with sprays of yellow flowers pluming from yellow turbans, circle, sing, and sway as village drums and flutes welcome spring.

Going around to the southeast of the tower, we look down at the monuments of the next dynasty, the Khilji Kings. Below is a small building that sparkles like a jewel box. Carved red sandstone makes its walls, white filigreed marble its windows. It is the Alai Darwaza—Gatehouse of Alai—built in 1310.

Certainly splendor and refinement were in the man Ala-ud-Din Khilji, next important sultan of Delhi and most powerful Khilji king; but to the north a hulking mound of stone—the Alai Minar—speaks loudly of his mad ambition. Brilliant and arrogant, jealous, suspicious, and utterly cruel, Ala's grandiose scheme succeeded. He brought all India under his sway, and his armies staggered back to Delhi under loads of loot. Six hundred and twelve elephants and 20,000 horses carried 3,840,000 pounds of pure gold and 20,000 pounds of jewels—diamonds, pearls, emeralds, and rubies—from just one expedition to the South.

Delirious from this successful violence, Ala-ud-Din roared: "I am the second Alexander," and dreamed of conquering the world. To crown his spectacular and terrible reign, he planned a minar twice as big as the minar of Qutb. But his unrestrained way of life took its toll: that unfinished heap—the Alai Minar—is all that came of

The Alai Minar

it. To the north a pattern of rubble marks his extensive additions to Rai Pithora. He renamed the whole enlarged capital Siri. It is the third city of Delhi.

The dark stairs of the Qutb Minar lead up. Thirty-six steps to another balcony; then up 30 more. We step into blinding sun and survey the world from a platform 10 feet in diameter and 234 feet in the air. We are at the top of the tallest free-standing stone tower in the world. After six hundred years we have followed the builder of these two highest sections of the tower. In 1370 Firoz Shah, third king of the Tughluq Dynasty, climbed eagerly to see the heartland of his kingdom.

To the east he saw a colossal rampart like a scooped-out mountain spreading over a high ledge of rock. It is Delhi's fourth city, Tughluqabad, dynastic citadel of the Tughluq Sultans. Ghias-ud-Din Tughluq, soldier of fortune, founded the dynasty, and built that great bastion in two years. Once a scene of haunting savage splendor—"built," writes a chronicler, "of gilded bricks which shone so dazzlingly that none would gaze steadily upon it"—it is now a ruined mass. But what a spectacle of medieval might it was—a golden city crouching in the sun on these bare brown hills.

Near it on a rock island, in what was then a spreading lake but is now fields and pastures, is the powerfully designed fort-tomb of old Ghias-ud-Din. The plain red sandstone and white marble walls, almost Egyptian in form, are so slanted-in that wild green parrots swoop down to rest, clinging against the high walls, screaming to one another. Strangely untouched by the forces that pulled

The ruins of Tughluqabad

Tomb of Ghias-ud-Din, still intact

down the city, it is a monument worthy of the sturdy and venerated soldier-king buried there.

Ruined walls and archways stand on the hills beyond Tughluqabad. These are eloquent reminders of impossible plans. Muhammad Tughluq, second sultan of the dynasty, was at times almost a saint. Certainly he was an intellectual genius, but all his virtues were undone by a temper so violent that he could act like a mad man.

Fearing the Mongols, who were ravaging the world, he enclosed Siri and Tughluqabad in one huge city—Delhi's fifth—and named it Jahanpanah, World's Refuge. This was accomplished with great effort on the part of his people. As soon as it was done, he suddenly decided the capital would be safer seven hundred miles south. But the people were reluctant to leave their ancestral homes. Muhammad was so enraged that he force-marched the entire population *en masse* to the new city. Many died of fatigue on the way. The rest were unhappy in new surroundings. Realizing his mistake, Tughluq ordered everyone back to Delhi. On the return trip, thousands of the desperate citizens, worn out and disheartened, died by the wayside. He came back to a ruined capital and a demoralized kingdom.

When Muhammad died, Firoz Shah—on whose pinnacle-platform we stand—became sultan of what was left of Delhi. This man was too gentle to be king in those times. The nobles, many of the princely Turkish blood, enforced their policies and preferences by strong-arm methods, or by poison and dagger. The Mongols ravaged the border. But Firoz Shah loved the arts of peace and disliked the arts of war. Although Delhi and the inner kingdom prospered, the empire, under his kind rule, began to disintegrate.

From this top platform we pay homage to his achievements. He wrote: "Among the gifts which God bestowed on me, his humble servant, was a desire to erect public buildings." And he did: mosques without number, five fortified cities, the restoration of historical monuments.

The sun urges descent from these historic heights. Ten miles away, but seen clearly from here, the skyline of New Delhi invites us into the present times. Grasping the handrail, we slowly return to earth.

The garden is crowded as it always is. Mothers and fathers sit on the lawn; children play in the shadow of the great tower. For over seven hundred years, this slender minaret has stood against the clear sky, the white and dusty-rose of its sandstone brightening at noon, softening as evening comes.

Turning left from the highway to Delhi, a little side road runs smoothly west over fields ridged and jagged with mounds of stone, once part of Siri. Sun-bleached, age-defaced tombs, defiant of time, are hunched on rocky knolls. The scene is rugged, bleak beyond description. Here one feels the austere, aggressive nature of those earliest Turkish sultans. What grace they had was, like the obliterated ornament of these tombs, merely surface decoration. Their business was to fight, conquer, and rule, to carve kingdoms from hostile lands.

But now the countryside softens. A trace of green shows where underground water nears the surface. Trees and shrubs appear, and houses. The car stops before a tall gate with trees and domes glimpsed beyond. It is just a step into a pleasant world, a world of serene lawn-carpeted silence, of simple pavilions—strong white columns poised on green grass. Walls reach out to enclose these acres. A wild peacock paces along the ridge of the wall, brushing the dark stones with his train of gorgeous feathers. Trees festoon the corners.

This is Hauz-Khas, the garden university built by Firoz Shah Tughluq as a seat of Arabic learning. White-robed teachers once taught in the shade of these pavilions or strolled with their students on the grass at dusk. It is so quiet that the sudden laugh of a little boy, playing on

Hauz-Khas, the garden university

the lawn, startles the peacock. It cries in its strange voice and sails over the wall, tail swept out behind.

There is another surprise. The path leads right. A raised stone plinth is backed by stone arches. Look through them. . . . There's nothing but air on the other side, straight down for forty feet. Peering cautiously, you see that this is the very edge of a high cliff. Cut into its face below, are rooms and colonnades opening on what is now a broad dry bowl of pasture land. In Firoz Shah's day it was a seventy-acre lake surrounded by trees. On the hottest day the air was fresh. In his beloved garden stands the beautiful tomb of Firoz Shah Tughluq.

In 1398, the Mongol scourge of the fourteenth-century world, Timur—the crippled Tamerlane the Terrible —camped on the shore of this peaceful lake after the sack of Delhi. His blood-drenched hordes rested from their brutalities under the trees. Herds of cows and buffaloes are placidly grazing there now; three young cowherds rest on the grass.

It is high noon. The mysteries of the pre-dawn drive are no more. Neat, white housing developments nudge the virile battlements of Siri, dispelling the ghosts of its many violent struggles for power.

We pass Safdarjung Airport where inland planes roar off, to follow by air the far-flung, ancient Delhi-centered roads. Traffic lights flash red and green, buses hold up loud-horned automobiles. We work our way through modern bedlam, down modern boulevards, spin up to the hotel door, hurry into "air-conditioned comfort"—our lives enriched by the history of Delhi.

III.

NEW DELHI

The monsoon rolls up to Delhi in mid-July. All day the clouds pile up, spirits rise, and by afternoon's first wild downpour the heat-weariness has vanished and everyone longs to rush out to greet the rain. A few minutes after the last drops, out they troop. Children splash into puddles; everyone laughs. They fill their lungs with the cool, washed air and watch one of the rainy season's special wonders—a breathtaking sunset. With a Midas touch it changes the universe into a realm of gold—streets, trees, people, the river, the Vista, its fountains, the great Capitol buildings, and the hill. . . . Air travelers, soaring up from Palam, press against the windows. They look down at New Delhi, India's great capital, and see a golden city spread on gold North Indian plains.

Like heroes lifted on the city's shoulders, the Capitol buildings rest in grandeur on Raisina Hill. Their red and fawn-white stones, radiant in daylight, slumber at night with a dark glow. Far down the long lawn of the Vista, just east of India Gate, a statue of George V, king of England, gazes intently at them through the great arch.

In 1911 the English sovereigns, as Emperor and Empress of India, visited Delhi. North of Old Delhi, where it was thought Indra Prasthna had stood, a glittering public reception swirled around them for days. At this Great Durbar, George V declared Delhi the capital of India. A new city would be built, a New Delhi—the last, the greatest.

The king and queen sailed west again and plans got under way. Britain's outstanding architects—both knighted later—hurried to India: Edwin Lutyens from England, Herbert Baker from Africa. But where should the new city stand? After months of indecision, Lord Hardinge, the Viceroy, mounted his horse one morning and galloped over the plains. Near Raisina Village he found a hill in the scrub jungle. "From the top," he writes, "there was a magnificent view embracing old Delhi and all the principal monuments situated outside the town, the Yamuna winding like a silver streak in the foreground. . . . I said at once: 'This is the site for Government House.' "

Statue of King George V of England, as seen through India Gate

New Delhi traffic, rushing across the city, revolves around this acropolis and its symbolic echo, India Gate. Except for Janpath, the important streets all stem from them and from Connaught Place. The core of the city is a sharp tree-and-macadam triangle pointing due north: Connaught Place the tip; Curzon Road and Parliament Street the sides; and the mile-long processional boulevard, Rajpath, the base. Rajpath strikes west from India Gate, bisects Central Vista, widens round water-bright fountain pools at Great Place, climbs Raisina Hill between impressive twin Secretariats designed by Baker, and, sweeping down a sunken drive, rises into the dramatic Entrance Courtyard of Lutyen's masterpiece, Rashtrapati Bhavan, formerly the Vice-Regal Palace.

This beautiful, shadow-striped building is the Presi-

The twin Secretariats

dent's House. Majestically imaginative, it inspired a famous architect to say: "Who but Lutyens would put fountains on the roof!" It took years to build. As for the earlier Delhis, marble and sandstone had to be laboriously brought from remote quarries in Rajasthan. Master masons and an army of stone workers toiled directly under Lutyens, who had traveled all over India studying the ancient architecture before designing this proud-domed, masculine palace.

From a labyrinth of regal Rooms of State, lustrous with white marble, red brocade, and gold, two small plain rooms were chosen as the President's private suite. Among his books, and the pictures of Mahatma Gandhi, he ponders India's mammoth dreams, writes historic treatises, and receives his callers. A distinguished dedicated Head of

Rashtrapati Bhavan, the President's house

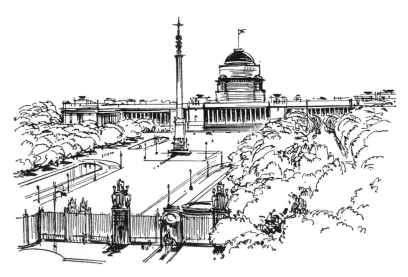

Indian Gardens, west of the President's house

State—in India the Prime Minister is the administrative head—the President occasionally gives public audiences. His Military Secretary arranges them. Visitors enjoy a tour of these fine corridors, admiring the beautiful details and decorations and especially the attendants in their colorful dress. Passes are issued right at the building.

Famous Indian Gardens full-blooming in late winter, west of the Bhavan, are a fairyland of pools and water-courses. On the emerald lawns, fountains splash. Flower-covered terraces surround a sunken pool. During October, when Diwali, the Festival of Lights, sparkles over India, this lovely garden and the serene over-shadowing facade, festooned with strings of twinkling, incandescent lights, spell pure enchantment.

Just outside the North Gate of the President's House is a tall beige-stone building, austere and dignified. It is the Anglican Cathedral, Church of the Redemption. Lord Irwin, the Viceroy, and Lady Irwin gave the east-wall painting to commemorate their escape from an assassin's bomb. Christianity was not, as might be thought, brought to India by Europeans. Deep in the green countryside of South India little bands recount a long tradition. The gospel, they say, was brought to India by St. Thomas in 52 A.D.

South Avenue begins at the Bhavan's South Gate, passes apartment houses where members of Parliament live, and ends at the Prime Minister's tree-concealed mansion. East of Raisina Hill lies the wonderful green, sun-rich sweep of Central Vista. Edging the formal beauty of fountains and trees are many buildings. Most are massive government offices. But two are of special interest.

Parliament House, nearest the Hill, is a handsome red-stone building with white columns, as round as the Wheel of Order of India's national emblem. It is the place of a historic scene—the signing at midnight on August 14, 1947, of the document that created modern India and Pakistan. Great debates take place during sessions of the Raj Sabha and Lok Sabha, Upper and Lower Houses of Parliament. When the Prime Minister speaks, visitors' galleries are packed with intense citizens and fascinated travelers. The nation's business is done in two languages used interchangeably—Hindi, a Sanskrit-based North-Indian language, and English, a British legacy and one of India's greatest international assets.

The National Museum, halfway down the Vista on Janpath, and opposite the National Archives, is a Delhi

The Anglican Cathedral, Church of the Redemption, at right; Parliament House, below

The National Museum

highpoint. Handsome carved and brass-studded doors lead to world-famous marvels of Indian art. Tourists keyed to bright sun and speed stride up the steps. But a hushed, timeless atmosphere imposes a slower tempo as they pace through these beautiful galleries. The great Mathura Buddha stands serenely circled by the radiant disk of his stone halo. A small Mogul beaker—of fragile, gold-etched, lime-green glass—dreams of the scent of Persian roses. There are rare South Indian bronzes and kings' jewels: great uncut diamonds, emeralds lying like green lakes in valleys of heavy gold. There are an exquisite scrap of vine-embroidered gold brocade, last silk memory of a prince's wedding coat; a crescent sword, jeweled hilt glinting coldly; and a bronze shield, helmet, and spear, inlaid with gold and silver—menacing tools of a vanished warrior-king. The museum continues to grow, as new treasures are acquired under the guidance of Dr. Grace McCann Morley, an outstanding American museologist, chosen by India as the first National Director of Museums.

The Mathura Buddha

On down the Vista, Prince's Park stems out around tall India Gate like a giant, green, six-petaled flower. Elegant princely palaces, all now converted to public use, are reminders of grandiose British days. Jaipur House is the National Gallery of Modern Art, and worth a visit, to see the paintings by Shergil.

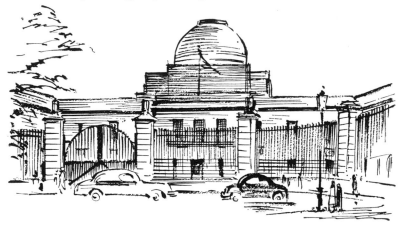

Jaipur House, the National Gallery of Modern Art

71

The President's bodyguard

Two recent buildings terminate the Vista tour: the Supreme Court on Tilak Marg, and the National Stadium built across the eastern end in 1950. Purana Qila and the Yamuna River, intended by Lutyens to be its grand and glorious finale, are cut off from the Vista by the stadium.

India enjoys a week of pride and celebration beginning every January 26. The Republic was born in 1948 on that day. Along Rajpath, Delhi's triumphal route, rolls the colorful Republic Day Parade. Seats are much in demand for the spectacle. It is certainly the nation's grandest. Everybody who can squeeze in is there. Westerners wear head coverings for those hours of winter sun.

Down from the President's House, across Great Place and on between grandstands, crammed with excited, holidaying people, two troops of turbaned, red-and-gold-uniformed horsemen—the President's bodyguard—trot swiftly on magnificent white horses. Between them a carriage, drawn by prancing blacks, carries a dignified man shaded by a gold-fringed umbrella, a *Chattra*, ancient Indian symbol of government. The cavalcade swings up to the reviewing stand. The guardsmen raise bannered trumpets. There is a brass-throated blare. The President of India has arrived.

Waves of dress-parading troops strut down Rajpath, bands playing. Tartaned bagpipers with tiger-skin capes flaunt along to their own jaunty wail. A Camel Corps, India's desert fighters, stalk superciliously past. Planes zoom overhead, a helicopter sprinkles rose petals on the crowd. Elephants—gold-masked, painted, brocade-draped, their broad backs heaving like an ocean liner's dance floor —are merely ornamental now, but armored elephants were once the fighting tanks of India. And, finally, elaborate Floats of the States depict the nation's fascinating diversity. It is a day of wonderful hunting for camera-carriers.

In the evening, people, bundled in coats and shawls,

The President of India arrives, shaded by a Chattra

One of the Floats of the States

carrying blankets—for winter nights are cold—pour into
the stadium for the National Folk Dances. Now the vast
stadium goes dark. A humming silence falls on fifty thousand people. Suddenly a wild, electrifying tribal shout
and a spotlight together ignite a small holocaust in the
center of the dark arena. Some of these dances, anthro-
pologists say, are more than five thousand years old. To
Americans the Manipuri Nagas dancers—one-time head
hunters of Assam—seem much like the American Indians,
with feathered headdresses, breech-clouts woven in zig-
zags of black, white, and red, and bows and arrows, leaping in a circular, hopping war dance and singing a high,
keening song.

It is an astonishing fact that each stage of human history—prehistoric, archaic, barbaric, feudal, medieval—
flourishes in some corner of modern India. For example:
New Delhi people gather under a Shamyana tent late on

a winter night to see a traditional South Indian dance drama—Kathakali. The only light—a center-stage, erratic flame of oil, on its tall brass pedestal—casts a suggestive play of shadows against the black-striped, red Shamyana. The drummers begin. This three-hundred-year-old classical drama of the world of gods and demons is performed by men trained rigorously from boyhood. In towering elaborate masks—red or black or green—grotesque costumes fantastically puffed and padded to supernatural proportions, the dancers re-enact the unearthly dramas—cruel and inscrutable—of Good and Evil. Gestures are

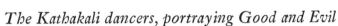

The Kathakali dancers, portraying Good and Evil

styled into an elaborate symbolism without words but with screams, chirps, bellows, and roars. The super-charged atmosphere is a remarkable experience to anyone who enjoys bizarre effects.

A moment of spine-chilling beauty ends a week of national festivities. At sunset, in the grandeur of Great Place, the bands of all the Forces merge in an ancient military ritual: massed, heart-shaking drum-thunder, hushed to a whisper as the sun dies—the beating of Retreat.

Picturesque, ruined red-stone walls loom southeast of India Gate. Called Lal Durwaza, they are the outer bastion of Purana Qila. Beyond them stand the tumbling, but still majestic ramparts of the old citadel. Lutyens prophetically angled the Vista to include Purana Qila, not knowing that in 1953 fragmented bricks and potsherds of Indra Prasthna would be found under it. He linked, with a strip of park land, the buried first city and the soaring new, closing a circle of history three thousand years long.

Imposing gates, studded with white marble and blue enamel, proudly guard the grand memories of Purana Qila. It is thrilling to enter this romantic fortress that fairly breathes medieval pageantry and splendor, all powerfully enclosed by the grim, decaying gray walls. Now a popular National Park, this mass of stone had a strange part to play in the life of the second Mogul King, Humayun.

The first Mogul—the word is a contraction of Mongol —was the tough, elegant Persian, Babur, Humayun's father whose *Memoirs* have been translated into Eng-

*Lal Durwaza above; the imposing gateway
to Purana Qila below*

lish. His army poured from Persia through the Hindu Kush, dragging cannons and guns, then unknown in India. He defeated Ibrahim Lodi and conquered Delhi in 1526, thus founding the Dynasty of Grand Moguls. Violent blood rushed through Babur's veins: his father was descended from the dreaded Timur, his mother from Ghengis Khan, the world-ravaging Tartar. A century before Babur, vandal hordes of these two destroyers, raging in the Middle East, forced Europe, cut off by land from Asia's luxuries, to hazard an improbable, western, world-shaking new route to India. But this ominous ancestry gave to Babur (and to his Grand Mogul descendants) its wealth of Tartar vigor and keenness, Persian elegance and subtlety.

When Babur died, Humayun secured the throne, but preferred harem intrigues to affairs of state. He learned his lesson when the Afghan Sher Shah drove him into exile. For fifteen years Humayun shuttled between neighboring rulers, begging for military help. There were two bright spots in those dangerous years in the Sind desert—marriage to Hamida, a Sindi princess; and, in 1542, the birth of his son Akbar, destined for great things.

Just before he lost Delhi, Humayun laid foundations for a new city, Din Panah, Abode of the Modest, completed by Sher Shah. We call it Purana Qila, the Old Fort. It is the seventh city of Delhi.

The stones of Purana Qila fairly ripple as sun strikes their exquisite carvings. The citadel was designed in splendid Afghan style, a blend of Hindu and Persian motifs. Wide stone steps in the center court lead deep

*Sher Shah's Mosque above;
Sher Mandal below*

into an echoing well. There were underground baths, shimmering caverns of cool, rose-scented water where the royal harem sported and splashed on scorching midsummer days. Two buildings —Sher Shah's Mosque, a gem of design, and the small Sher Mandal—are the last lonely witnesses of that palatial city. Wise, kingly Sher Shah had little time to enjoy his achievement. In 1545 an accidental explosion of gunpowder killed him. Quarreling successors soon demoralized the kingdom and Humayun, helped by the Persian king, reconquered Delhi. Striding into the usurper's capital he climbed to the Mandal's upper room and reclaimed Din Panah and his kingdom. Six months later that little building destroyed him. Descending the stairs, he slipped on a broken step, fell, and, mortally injured, soon died.

Under the Old Fort's lifeless walls a little thatch-roofed village has taken shape. Refugees sheltering there built huts and planted a tulsi bush—quaint symbol of home and fidelity. In a time-honored Indian parable, wealth, beauty, position, and learning are outweighed on the divine scales by a sprig of tulsi. The plants are lovingly tended and even worshiped by the simple village women.

Purana Qila's villagers are not alarmed when tigers growl and lions roar near them. The modern zoo, just south, is alive with splendid inhabitants: both exotic and familiar beasts and birds. Their jungle sounds delight residents of neighboring Sundar Nagar, a colony of two-story, two-apartment houses named for the Municipal Horticultural Gardens nearby.

But there is not much of Delhi's special charm in the newer parts of town. The houses, close together and almost alike, were hurriedly built for renting, and the rents are high. After India's independence, foreign governments and firms, pressed by rapid expansion, leased the houses for their staffs. Trees in the small squares will eventually veil the hard facades. Little pocket-handkerchief gardens and roof decks make them comfortable. Often well furnished, the rooms may be bright with copper and brass pieces bought from nearby Sundar Nagar bazaar by an enthusiastic *memsahib*, wife of a *sahib*, an educated man. This title, applied to both Indians and foreigners, is a great distinction in a place where most have no hope of higher schooling.

Although Delhi is an international crossroads, very few of its two million inhabitants are foreigners. Even with

Shrine of Nizam-ud-Din

the Diplomatic Corps, there are only about five thousand Western people who call New Delhi home. Their way of life is not much different from that of the well-to-do Indians who make up the bulk of the capital's citizenry. At the occasional performances of touring Western musicians or actors, the audience is largely Indian. They, and the Western tourists, are the patrons of the night clubs, restaurants, and hotels that are like such places anywhere in the world. The foreigners who live in Delhi usually entertain in their homes.

Several residential districts were developed in New Delhi during the 1950's. Five miles south of Sundar Nagar on Mathura Road is Friend's Colony, a garden suburb. The beautiful tournament-standard golf course has christened an overbuilt namesake, a district called Golf Links. An old Mogul Garden—Jor Bagh—has been replaced with houses. Nizam-ud-Din, named for a local saint whose ornate little shrine shares a fascinating enclosure with other filigreed tombs, was once a village. And Lodi Estates is quite unlike the romantic Lodi Gardens, a graceful wilderness that invites a ramble.

High round domes, like huge moons, over the Lodi Garden trees speak of a time after Firoz Shah Tughluq when weak or blundering kings—but masters of murder and treachery—swaggered up in turn for a disordered hour on Delhi's tottering throne. The people despaired. During those shifting moods of history, macabre thoughts flourished like blooms of death and dissolution. Gardens of tombs sprang up around the city in cemeteries—called *maqbarah*, an Arabic word that begot our word *macabre*. Built while their future tenants lived, the tombs, surrounded by lawns and flowers, were garden houses, picnic spots for family parties, until permanently occupied. In the Lodi Garden tombs sleep Turkish Sayyid kings and the Afghan Lodis who ruled before Babur.

After Humayun's untimely death, Akbar, a boy of fourteen, was crowned king. His mother, Hamida, asked for the realm's greatest architect to design her husband's tomb. In a little town built just for her, she watched for eight years as ruby-red stones rose to become the brooding shadow-slashed Humayun's Tomb, one of Delhi's show places.

Hamida's intelligent influence helped her son to become Akbar the Great. And great he was—one of the greatest geniuses of all time. Powerful, flashing-eyed, a lover of sports, Akbar looked every inch a king in the excitement of a cheetah hunt, or striding through his mag-

Humayun's Tomb

nificent palace to the royal seraglio and his thousand
queens. He brushed aside traditional ways, developed new
methods of government, a new spirit in art, poetry, music,
and religion. Thinkers and artists from far lands added
brilliance to his court. Near Agra, at Sikandra-bad, herds
of deer bound through the shady park surrounding his
beautiful tomb.

But Fatehpur Sikri, twenty miles away in the desert,
is his masterpiece. Cresting a cliff, the high-walled, glowing red city has been perfectly, almost magically pre-
served in the clear, hot, echo-haunted air. Once dancing
girls stood in the courtyard's inlaid chessboard squares,

living pawns for kingly games of chess. Now wild peacocks stroll in the deserted courts, where once rich,
imperial throngs lived out the dramas since immortal-
ized by generations of roving puppeteers. Every winter,
these gypsy-like people come to Delhi. Then modern children squeal with delight as garish little Rajasthan puppets
swing giddily through miniature adventures from those
fantastic days.

Where Lodi Road and Qutb Road meet, stands Safdar
Jung's Tomb, the stilted last building in the Mogul manner. Blooming rows of lavender jacaranda trees frame the
red-coral walls in early summer. It is a favorite place for
an evening stroll, this lacy garden with the prim, sweetly
charming tomb, a valentine of red and white stones. And
overhead, sleek planes slant down for a landing at Safdar-
jung Airport.

Smart racetrack and polo crowds cheer the winter
events at the Race Course and Gymkhana Club near Safdarjung. Racing, a Mogul passion, is also a favorite sport
with the modern descendants of horse-taming Aryans.
And in 1862, English tea planters, exploring the Hills (as
the Himalayas up to 13,000 feet are called), found tribal
Manipuris playing a dangerous game. Madly dashing on
tough, furry, half-wild ponies they thrashed the air and
each other with long sticks as they whacked at a hard,
fiber-stuffed and oiled leather ball. The game, Kangjai,
called Polo in Tibet, was brought to Calcutta sporting
fields and given rules. It is especially thrilling played by
daring Rajput Rajas of Udaipur, Jaipur, and Jodhpur

Akbar's tomb, near Agra, site of the Taj Mahal

Fatehpur Sikri

Safdar Jung's tomb

(our riding breeches of the same name are their regional garb) on the green polo fields of India.

From Murti Marg and the Prime Minister's house a small bridge spans a dry moat and beyond are the tree-lined boulevards of Diplomatic Enclave, area of foreign embassies. Officially called Chanakya Puri, it is named for Chanakya, India's most illustrious ancient Prime Minister. Exiled by the Greeks, Chanakya met in a forest a vigorous young brigand, Chandra Gupta Maurya, and appraised him as a leader who could rally India against Greek rule. In 313 B.C. Chanakya helped him to found the mighty Maurya Dynasty, to throw off the Greeks, and to conquer all of India but Kalinga, the modern state of Orissa; he was the first to unify the nation. The founder's grandson was the world-famous Ashoka. A ruthless fighter —legend says he slew ninety-nine half brothers in a grim free-for-all for the throne—Ashoka promptly invaded Kalinga.

The people fought like demons. As men fell, women and children heroically threw themselves against the invaders. They came raging up, with small weapons in their hands, to be crushed under Ashoka's war elephants. He conquered Kalinga, but the sights of the carnage shocked and transformed him. Renouncing war, he became a Buddhist, dedicating himself and his empire to the Law of Dharma—Self Understanding. Arms were destroyed. The Royal Hunt was abolished. Reverberating drums spoke no more of war but only of Dharma. In the royal kitchens that had curried a thousand peacocks and as many deer daily for the royal household and the priests, no living thing was permitted to be killed. Only fruits and curries of vegetables were served.

Every ten years, in a famous 256-day walk, Ashoka traversed India explaining morality, peace, and piety to his people. As reminders he raised the astonishing Ashoka columns engraved with the Laws of Right Conduct. The Lion capital from an Ashokan column is modern India's national emblem. Two of the columns are in Delhi (see page 103). Until Ashoka's death, in 244 B.C., India was ruled without arms or fear by his great edict, "Truth Alone Triumphs." Ashoka lives in legends and histories as a King-Colossus, to many historians the world's supreme monarch, towering above all others in breadth and nobility of mind, coupled with indomitable energy.

The Lion capital, India's national emblem

Travelers shade their eyes to gaze out from the high roof terraces of Delhi's impressive government-run Hotel

Government-run Hotel Ashoka

Ashoka. The winter light is luminous, distances deceptive. The pale sky and the flat, low-lying plain—only 720 feet above sea level—race away toward the shimmering far horizon. An exhilaration is in the air. Each point of the compass has a story to tell. South, Qutb Minar's tall finger marks that page of history; east, the Yamuna River flows past the sprawling twentieth-century capital, her patient energies molding even this latest Delhi; north, the splendid mass of the Capitol buildings rises in triumphant grandeur like a great magnet drawing together and welding into one nation the amazing diversities of India; and west, parallel to the guardian Ridge, spacious Diplomatic Enclave spells out modern history in the making.

Almost no one walks in Delhi; the distances, and the heat, are too great. In the Enclave, there seems to be an endless procession of cars and bicycles sliding along to the various Chanceries of the world. Down Shanti Path, the central boulevard, the foreign embassies are ranged in a fascinating display of national characteristics.

Crossing the Enclave, Panchsheel Marg passes, among others, the white-and-gold American Embassy and auxiliary buildings, to end at Sardar Patel Road, the Palam Airport highway. Gray-green jungle trees droop gracefully north of the highway. On the south side, there are large new private homes representing the modern but truly Indian architectural form that has developed.

Sardar Patel Road joins Willingdon Crescent; the Crescent circles west around Raisina Hill to Irwin Road. Handsome red sandstone gates and walls, enclosing the President's estate, give distinction to this curving boulevard. In the estate a park-like wealth of trees and gardens are shared by the mansions of cabinet ministers and the small homes of the Bhavan's maintenance staff.

Side streets lead off Willingdon Crescent to the National Laboratory, to experimental farm sites and institutes for much-needed rural redevelopment, to a big new Hindu temple (Lakshmi Narayan), and to lovely Talkatora Gardens. This Mogul park is a mecca for camera enthusiasts for weeks before Republic Day when excited folk-dancers camp there and rehearse in the morning sunshine.

The American Embassy

Lakshmi Narayan, the new Hindu temple

From the Roman Catholic Cathedral of the Sacred Heart, Irwin Road rolls past an eye-catching fruit bazaar, piled high with luscious Indian fruits, to Connaught Place.

In India, the symbol of summer is fruit. Indian trees yield marvels all year long: loose-skinned winter oranges; fresh *leeches*—red-brown, dragon-skinned, and filled with a slip-out, grape-sweet pulp; custard apples like vanilla puddings in medieval, bronze-green, armored balls. Apples, pears, peaches, grapes, and plums come from Kashmir, Kulu Valley, the Simla Hills, and from the Nilgiri (Blue) Mountains where Indian beer is brewed. And

Scene in Talkatora Gardens, showing rehearsal of folk dancers

Fruit sellers in the fruit bazaar

always bananas—wonderful *kay-la*—from tiny, three-inch plump fingers to great dark-red clubs. Poorer train travelers survive for days on the ever-present milky-sweet tea and *kay-la*, hawked at every station from head baskets. There are little *cheekoos*—sweet, brown fruits that look like golf balls; delectable ice-green melons picked from vines clambering on the thatch of village roofs; papayas—orange-yellow, deliciously flower-scented, and filled with black, nasturtium-flavored seeds. But, as an Indian will tell you, all play second fiddle to the exotic, baffling, mighty mango. Like all masterpieces, a mango is a deceptive thing. Its flavor is strong and delicate, sweet, delicious, but pungent almost to rankness.

This parade of fruits brings crowds to the fruit bazaar. Men are the family shoppers. On the way home from work they stop, select, hand-weigh, haggle passionately, and march off in triumph and anticipation.

Also near Connaught Place, on Parliament Street,

Jantar Mantar

among the huge, new early-modern-style bank and business buildings, are the round All India Radio Building and a wonderful wizard's garden—a big, fantastic multi-colored mad maze called Jantar Mantar. Newcomers can never guess that it is an outdoor Solar Observatory. The weird but precisely scientific shapes were planned and built in 1723—before New Delhi was dreamed of—by the astronomer Maharaja of Jaipur.

All India Radio Building

Beginning deep in the trees of New Delhi's finest residential part, Janpath, the north-south avenue, skims quietly round landscaped circle intersections, crosses Central Vista, and begins to hum as the columns of the Central Post Office come into view. Nearing Connaught Place, it breaks into a lively tune of traffic and trade. Here, on the sidelines of this busy street, Tibetan traders sit under the trees, their curios spread on the footpath. Sturdy, quick-smiling, these women skillfully play the age-old game of overcharging tourists. They bargain with all their wiles—scornful, angry, and cajoling in turn.

Every autumn the same families trudge over the high Himalayan passes and come down to winter at Delhi. Husbands scour the rough Old Delhi bazaars for merchandise. The wives sell it to tourists in New Delhi. When footpath business is slow, some of the women may bundle their wares into a little one-horse, two-wheeled *tonga* cart and sashay off to the outskirts to ring foreigners' doorbells.

Their goods are genuine; some are even rare and valuable. But the pleasure is in the scene, one of the happiest in the city—intriguing displays spread on colored rugs, dappled and half-toned by tree-filtered sun: burnished copper, multicolored beads, small brass gods and whimsical animals crowded in silent conclave under tall, copper, silver-banded Tibetan horns, and, ensconced in the middle, picturesque smiling Junos, hair in braids, wearing ancestral necklaces of chunky turquoises, and striped pink aprons over black robes, their chubby babies rolling on a little rug nearby.

The man of the silk-weaving family, working a wide loom

Beyond the Tibetans, Janpath becomes a bedlam of tiny refugee shops. Planted on the footpath in 1947, they rooted and grew into a permanent row of shacks selling a cut-price medley of toothpaste, toys, and other odds and ends. Almost hidden behind these stalls the government Handicraft Emporium is suavely modern, heady with color, and as fabulous as any Oriental fantasy. Well-designed objects and fabrics are beautifully displayed.

All of Connaught Place is fascinating. Important jewelry shops have gems for sale that were collected by generations of princely families. In one steel-doored inner room, large, matched, pear-shaped, Oriental pearl earrings, worth a fortune, are hopefully shown to travelers. In another, Kashmir sapphires and diamonds are clustered into a great blue, dew-flecked rose.

In the sari shops a riot of colored cloth rages. No two of the six-yard, lustrous lengths are alike. Most of the saris are hand woven, and the people of a whole village may live by silk weaving. Women unwind the cocoons, children wash the threads for grandmothers to dye, men work with wide looms; streets pulse to the treadle's clacking.

Elaborate piece of hand-carved ivory

Kashmir woolen shawls of many colors and kinds appear. Famous Ring-shawls, the costly Shatush, woven of the soft fur from under the throat of wild, high-Himalayan goats, are so fine that a shawl four yards long and two wide will slide through a finger ring.

There are ivory shops, where chess sets of elephant-riding ivory maharajas, drawn up in battle array, glare across the chess board; book shops; shops of handmade shoes, with lovely hand-embroidered sandals; shops of rare antiquities: bronzes, stone figures, carpets (antique Persian and new Indian), prints, Mogul miniatures. Indian law requires that the Museum have first choice of all valuable stone and bronze pieces and dealers will supply clearance papers from the Department of Archaeology for the rarities they sell.

In the shadowy arcade fronting the shops an intense, turbaned man approaches a wide-eyed tourist. "You are very lucky. I tell your fortune. You get letter. Go away

96

soon." As the victim walks on, he follows, repeats his stock prophecy; then, with a shrug, turns away. A little shoe-shine boy appears, pointing accusingly at dusty shoes.

Suddenly a high-pitched drumming begins. With a disarming smile a monkey-man, ragged and pencil-thin, sidles up, thumping his little drum and dragging two bored over-dressed monkeys on leashes. "See the monkey! Monkey dance!" He drums louder and, there they go, crazily dancing ballroom-style together. They leap over and over each other grinning broadly. A small coin is all he wants to feed himself and his Simian partners; these friends live and work together. But he must constantly drill them—monkeys forget easily.

The bird-man displays the remarkable tricks of his tiny, painted, trained birds, and, out in the residential districts, awesome dancers, led by a muscular, quick-eyed man hulk up the street—the dancing bears. When an audience gathers, they stand—neck ropes taut—and dance, jumping stiffly together with waving paws. But their black, shaggy fur hides angry hearts. With a roar they may suddenly grapple, tearing and slavering at each other with guttural snarls. The man cuffs and kicks them into quiet, but the audience has scattered. The dance is over.

Of all the Indian sounds, the gourd-pipe fluting of the snake charmer is wildest, most haunting. Reedy, with a strange metallic richness, it is weird and tragic; perfectly suited to the charmer and to his snakes. He stalks by on the footpath, a tall, henna-stained apparition in turban and ragged clothes. Three or four lumpy bundles on his back will soon be gently lowered to the ground and a corner of

each cloth tossed back to show a basket's edge. The man
squats down. The flute begins again. Slowly from one
dark tunnel of cloth a thin head lifts and sways forward.
The snake coils out over the basket toward the man. Then
another, and, as the snakes come, the piping tenses into
solid sound until all are raised and swaying before him.
Quickly he thrusts a cloth at each. They strike, discharg-
ing their poison. Now, dazed with sound, they are coaxed

Snake charmers

98

to glide up his arms, across his shoulders, to coil around his neck, moving in smooth, numb ritual. A touchy moment—sudden movements or loud noises break the spell; they tighten or strike. The hooded cobra is too venomous for this act but is kept swaying, heart-shaped, false-eyed and deadly, at arm's length. Even dazed and fang-drained, if its lightning strike should connect with his hand, there could be mortal danger. Snake charmers always carry an antidote. Sometimes a sleek little mongoose, a creature dedicated to reptile slaughter, follows the man on a lead. The fight arranged between mongoose and snake will end in an enforced draw: the snake charmer needs them both in his business. And he has promised the Snake God and Goddess that no harm will come to his charges. At a yearly ceremony the snakes are released. New ones are caught and the promise to the Snake Divinities is renewed.

Connaught Place is the center for travel agencies. They supply cars and experienced guides for side trips and spur-of-the-moment excursions. Airline offices, banks, movie houses, and popular Western-food restaurants are here. Public drinking is banned in Delhi so there are no cocktail bars. The Indian Government Tourist Information Service has a convenient office, but everyone in this cosmopolitan capital is quick to help bewildered newcomers.

Two main throughfares lead toward Old Delhi—Minto Road and Barakhamba Road. Cutting through a large middle-class section, Minto Road goes north to Circular Road, relic of City-Wall days. A mile-long *maidan*—public greensward—is the Ramleela Grounds where the Rama

Paper effigies of King Ravanna and his brothers

Plays are held. In 200 B.C. the legend of Ram was already an ancient hero-saga, its episodes carved in stone relief. The Ramayana is still big news to small fry on grandmother's knee. Every village has the plays. Indian children act out the Rama story the way American children play Cowboys and Indians. In the autumn, Delhi puts on a magnificent version of the play, climaxed uproariously by the burning of enormous paper effigies of the Demon King Ravanna and his horrible brothers.

Barakhamba Road goes west to Mathura Road, past another middle-class district well hidden behind fine old houses and public buildings. Down a narrow lane in the midst of this crowded, but tidy section, is the small home of a famous Indian musician.

Battalions of sandals and shoes, spread around his door, tell that a well-known singer of *bhajans*—Hindu holy songs—is about to begin. Inside, the brightly lit room is all white. There is no furniture. On a white cloth, spread over the floor, the audience, in white saris or white shirts and trousers, is a dense mass—Indian people take pleasure in being close together. At the far end, seated on a wide white mat, the singer and her accompanists face the room. Stunning musical instruments of henna-colored, gleaming wood thrust an angular emphasis into the white space. Expressively, the singer lifts her face and, barely parting her lips, brings forth a thread of pure sound that soars, swells, dies. Poignant undertones from strings and drums carry the fabric of her song.

Indian classical singers (and all classical musicians) give themselves to music in their youth. It is a form of worship. Years of absolute discipline result in voices of almost uncanny flexibility and precision, capable of ranging, in the space of a downbeat, from a gossamer note, weaving swift, intricate webs of incredible beauty, to harsh gutturals—metallic, almost inhuman.

South on Mathura Road are permanent exhibition grounds. North, beyond Hardinge Bridge, the highway goes past a modern hospital and office buildings—significant new Indian architecture can be seen here—to the ruins of Firoz-abad, Firoz Shah Tughluq's fortified city.

At full glory, this sixth Delhi edged the river for six miles, from the Ridge to Indra Prasthna. After Firoz Shah's death, it was dismantled, stone by stone, for the buildings of lesser kings. Now children play and couples stroll on the grass around the ruined Royal Palace, the Kotla, said to have had three secret passages, long fallen in, but once wide enough to permit the carriages of royal ladies to speed unseen to the river or the hunting lodge, or even to the ancestral fortress at Rai Pithora. The old mosque is charred with age, the little royal swimming pool is dry, but on a pyramid of rough-stone terraces, once festooned with hanging gardens, a great shining shaft points forty-six feet into the blue sky.

This is one of Delhi's two famous Ashokan Pillars; the other is on the Ridge. No one today—skilled craftsmen, technicians, nor scholars—knows the secret of the column's polish. A lost art, apparently known only in Ashoka's time, gave to the pale, pink-gold sandstone a surface hard and brilliant as metal. Western Indologists first thought it *was* metal. The shaft, inscribed over two thousand years ago, seems freshly chiseled with Pali Script, a dead language deciphered only in 1837 by an Englishman, James Princep. It lists the seven moral guides, the Pillar Edicts of Ashoka.

Firoz Shah, eager to make his city the grandest Delhi, did not hesitate to send out teams of men with special rafts and forty-two-wheeled wagons to bring these twenty-seven-ton monuments to Delhi from Amballa and Meerut where they had stood for sixteen hundred years.

*The ruined Royal Palace, the Kotla, showing one of the
two famous Ashokan Pillars*

Mathura Road and Circular Road join at the garden circle where Delhi Gate stands. But before we enter the Old City, there is a small shrine to visit. It is Rajghat, the shrine of Mahatma Gandhi. Distinguished visitors come here to lay wreaths in homage. Twice a year devoted followers gather for an hour of silent, ritual spinning, in his memory. (See picture, page 31.)

This frail, practical visionary led India to independence. He brought about far-reaching social laws: the rights of women; legal abolition of caste taboos; division of absentee landlord estates among the poor tenant farmers. Discarding modern dress and ways of life—he was a successful, England-educated lawyer—Ghandi walked through the villages in peasant's clothes, preaching self-reliance. He taught the people to spin, to make their own cloth, to stand on their own feet. He embodied the finest ideals of ancient India and advanced as-yet-untried concepts of basic economics.

Placed between the Old City and the New, this shrine is like a double-acting hinge that keeps traditional India's door swinging wide to welcome new India, and keeps new India aware of its rich past. Mahatma Gandhi is truly called the Father of the Nation.

OLD DELHI

When the sun lies hot on Delhi and every shadow is a treasure, a wealth of deep gloom fills the long, covered arcade of Lahori Gate, the Red Fort's impressive western entrance. Idlers rest in the cool half light. A few beggars whine half-heartedly. Guides gossip in low voices, waiting for business. Tourists bargain for trinkets in the little shops installed in the thirty-two ornamental arches of the great gateway.

Three centuries ago, Shah Jahan ruled his flourishing kingdom from this magnificent riverside fortress. He planned and built both city and citadel. He was a Grand Mogul indeed, fifth of the dynasty and, under him, Indian imperial life reached unprecedented splendor. In his time, the little arcade shops of the Fort glittered with the richest wares of the East. Turbaned merchants, great rings flashing on several fingers, spread lavish displays to tempt the proud nobility entering this city within a city. The Fort's crenelated red-stone walls and towers enclosed a galaxy of gorgeous houses and palaces as well as barracks, bazaars, elephant stables, and a zoo. And west

The Red Fort

The "Seat of God's Shadow" in the Hall of Public Audience, Diwan-i-Am

of the citadel, Old Delhi—the eighth Delhi, then called Shahjahanabad—prospered in the shadow of these walls.

Much of the Fort is in ruins now. Invading Marathas and Persians stripped it of portable treasures. But for visitors, its past grandeurs come to life when they walk toward the Royal Drum House. Three hundred years ago a deafening clamor of drums, horns, and flutes would have welcomed them; the volume of the hullabaloo depending on the visitor's rank. Only the Emperor and Princes of the Royal Blood could ride under Drum House Gate. Whatever his rank, everyone else dismounted and, with suitable pomp, walked through to the Audience Courtyard and into the stately red-stone Diwan-i-Am, Hall of Public Audience.

Each morning, for two hours, the Emperor sat there and dispensed justice to all who came. Today's visitors look up at the "Seat of God's Shadow," a high marble throne-alcove, decorated with gems in fanciful Florentine designs by a renegade Italian artificer. They can imagine the handsome Emperor sitting there. He leans impressively forward to speak; then, work finished, he stands. Brocades and jewels fairly hiss in the rich shadows as he and his courtiers walk from the Public Hall into his shimmering private domain.

At twenty, Shah Jahan married beautiful, accomplished Mumtaz Mahal. When she died, after their nineteen years of rare happiness, he built Agra's incomparable Taj Mahal as her tomb.

Shah Jahan's was an enchanted, light-drenched world, edged by the shining river and open to the sky. Lawns, interlinked by a clear brook, called the Stream of Paradise, singing fountains, cascades, waterfalls, and reflecting pools made a green and silvery setting for palaces of dazzling white marble. An elegant throng of dark-eyed nobles, dignitaries, and royalty, gaily caparisoned servants, peacocks, doves, and pet deer mixed and moved through the marble halls and among the countless flowers. The Moguls were flower worshipers. Their lavishly blooming gardens were echoed by floral decorations on furniture, walls, floors, and clothes. The park-like grounds were dotted with marble pavilions. The Pavilion of the Summer Rains and the Pavilion of the Autumn Rains graced secluded gardens. The Life-giving Garden was a jewel-colored marvel of Persian roses steeped with Delhi's brilliant sun. In the Garden of Moonlight only scented white flowers grew. Nights, hushed and radiant under the full moon, enticed Shah Jahan and his beloved Queen, Mumtaz Mahal, into the Moonlight Garden. Resting on musk-

The Pearl Mosque

scented cushions and Persian carpets, they sipped spiced, sweet juices from jeweled goblets. Fountains splashed as musicians filled the luminous night air with festoons of silver sound, the famous moon-music.

Wonders are on all sides in the Red Fort: gorgeous marble bathing pools, including two charming small ones for the sport of royal children, the water ingeniously heated to different temperatures; the Pearl Mosque, its surprising luster heightened by afternoon sun; little Choice-Palace, now used as a museum. It houses collections of Mogul coins, a few paintings, weapons, and pieces of Chinese Celadon. Celadon bowls were much prized by the suspicious Moguls because poisoned food was supposed to crack them with a loud, warning report.

Diwan-i-Khas, the Palace-pavilion, Shah Jahan's Private Audience Hall

From the northeast corner of the citadel's sixty-foot wall, a heavy stone bridge arches out over Delhi's Ring Road, where water once flowed, to a dark stone prison of sinister legends.

Crowning the Red Fort's glories is a perfect example of Mogul design: the poetic white marble Palace-pavilion, Diwan-i-Khas, Shah Jahan's Private Audience Hall.

If there is a paradise on earth
It is here, it is here, it is here . . .

The words of the Persian couplet are carved high on an arch.

Every part of the Diwan-i-Khas is white. The ceiling is a shadowy, white inlaid heaven upheld by rows of massive, jeweled white piers. They branch up like a marble forest arching into a ripple-edged succession of flowing, gilded curves. The sun strikes a rim of satin-white floor. Tossed from the white surfaces, the reflected sunlight fills the Pavilion's cool depths with a delicate opalescence. Exquisitely designed to set off a lustrous chiaroscuro of pastel brocades, gold, and jewels, the Pavilion was the dazzling culmination of the extravagant world of luxury, the Oriental world of sumptuous splendor that surrounded Shah Jahan.

In the Diwan-i-Khas stood the fabulous Peacock Throne glowing like a jeweled rainbow in the cloud-white pavilion. Seven years in the making, valued at the equivalent of thirty-six million dollars, the throne was the Royal Divan of the Evening Court. It was sometimes carried for special durbars to the Diwan-i-Am. Six feet long, four feet wide, and luxuriously cushioned, the Peacock Throne stood on six solid-gold, jeweled leg-columns. Emerald-paved gold pillars supported a canopy of solid-gold, lavishly jeweled and richly fringed with fine pearls. A parrot, carved from a single huge emerald, swung down from the canopy on a jeweled perch. And full-spread across the back glittered two solid-gold peacocks entirely inlaid with gems, a blinding glory of deepest colors and radiance. An enormous chunk of pure rock-crystal almost as big as the throne lay near—huge, unflawed, a polished giant prism invaded by fleeting colors from the jeweled divan.

Seated on his glittering throne, robed in richest brocades, Shah Jahan wore on his cloth-of-gold turban a still more incredible gem, the diamond named Koh-i-Noor, "Mountain of Light." Then weighing 911 carats, it was the prize of the Mogul collection of world-famous Indian diamonds mined at Golconda, pre-African source of important stone.

In 1739 the Persian invader, Nadir Shah, defeated

Shah Jahan   *Rang Mahal*

an ineffectual Mogul king. Standing with sword in hand
before the little mosque, midway on Chandni Chowk, Old
Delhi's main street, the Persian massacred Delhi citizens as
fast as his soldiers could shove them up. After some thousands had been killed, his aching arm forced him to rest.
Later that day, in a parley with the defeated king, Nadir
Shah cunningly effected a trick exchange of turbans and
the Moguls lost the Koh-i-Noor. Now a fraction of its
original size, the diamond rests among other British Crown
Jewels in the Tower of London. The Peacock Throne,
taken to Persia by Nadir Shah, was broken up and melted
down.

From the Diwan-i-Khas, it is a step to the Women's
Pavilion, the Seraglio called Rang Mahal, Palace of Color.
The Lotus Pool once sprayed veils of scented water; the
Scales-of-Justice Screen hid Royal Ladies watching bar-
baric animal fights staged below in the riverside arena.
Near the Seraglio were the Emperor's gorgeous suite of
rooms. A flight of narrow steps leads down to a marble,
gold-roofed pavilion projecting from the east wall. Every

112

morning Shah Jahan stood in this Dawn Pavilion to greet the rising sun and receive the salutations of his subjects.

Modern history gives the Dawn Pavilion new significance. From it, in 1911, George V of England looked across the submissive conclave of Indian dignitaries to his vision of Empire. From it, independent India's first Prime Minister, Jaharwalal Nehru, on the morning of August 16, 1947 announced to the cheering multitude gathered below that a new free day had dawned over this ancient land.

Prime Minister Nehru announces India's independence

Jama Masjid, Delhi's Friday Mosque

The Red Fort is not Shah Jahan's only Delhi master-piece. Three great white marble spheres swell into the sky southwest of the Fort, the silhouette of the Jama Masjid, Delhi's Friday Mosque. Some connoisseurs of Islamic architecture label it India's finest mosque. Adding to its sanctity are three sacred relics—a hair from the beard of the Prophet, his sandal, and his footprint in stone.

Friday is the Muslim Sunday, the day for morning prayers at the mosque. Wearing round black hats and dressed all in white, devout men swarm up the steps and wash their hands and feet in the outer court pool. Purified and barefooted (visitors must remove their shoes here as at Hindu temples), they gather in the inner court, facing Mecca in solemn kneeling rows, while the Mullah intones from the Holy Koran. Women come, too, but pray out of sight in little screened-off porches. During Mogul days Fridays were spectacular. The Royal Party arrived by elephant procession and the ceremonies were in keeping.

Another handsome mosque, the Fatehpuri Mosque, stands at the other end of Chandni Chowk, Street of Moonlight. Midway between this and the Fort, the gilded domes of the Sikh Gurdwara, House of Worship, brightens the workaday medley of the Chowk. Much in evidence, driving Delhi's taxicabs, the turbaned Hindu sect of Sikhs, like Samson, never cut their hair or shave. Steel bracelets and daggers are ritual ornaments always

Chandni Chowk, Old Delhi's main street

The other end of Chandni Chowk, with Fatehpuri Mosque
in the background

worn by these militant, one-time farmers of the Punjab.

Delhi has wisely green-belted the space between the Jama Masjid, the Fort, and an interesting, much rebuilt four-hundred-year-old Jain Temple. But the Old City presses close to the mosque's west gate. It is in this jigsaw huddle of shack-shops that adventurous curio-seekers stumble on their rarest finds. A narrow, dingy junk-lined shop, or dark basement, like a catch-all pocket in the city's old coat, may hide the fine bronze, carved brass, or the copper piece that experienced eyes will identify under the mask of grime it wears. Occasionally a treasure turns up at the Saturday Mela (Fair), near the mosque where anything from practically new hub-caps to old, lily-trumpet gramophones, from last year's crudest calendar-art to classic Mogul miniatures may be spread on the sidewalk.

A deafening din reigns in the big markets, especially in the one near the mosque and in Chandni Chowk. Hindi, the common language of India, is sharp-edged; merchants who have them keep radios at top volume to induce a carnival mood that will make shoppers eager to buy. Combined, and increased by the closeness of the walls, these sounds create the din that is so maddening to visitors.

But suddenly you come upon a slit between tall buildings. Immediately on entering it, startling quiet descends. A passage, perhaps four feet across, winds for a block or so, between high walls. Just wide enough to allow two people to pass each other, or a cow and a man, if the man presses against the wall, the tiny canyon is dim and cool. For a few minutes at noon the sun looks in; then it is shadowy again. Not a ghost of a whisper from the seething bazaar blows down this narrow corridor. The masonry walls deaden sound. Footsteps brush worn stones, voices seem hushed. It is clean. By common consent no rubbish is dropped here. If it were, it would quickly block this trickling, but continuous traffic.

The lane widens. Light reflects into it from an opening ahead. Voices are heard in quiet conversation as you step into a small, wall-locked square. Handsome entrances —doors to the buildings that rise high on all sides—ornament the irregular, five-sided space, the angles made by the little lanes.

Word spreads very quickly that foreign visitors have arrived, and smiling people begin to appear. Children run out, jumping with the pleasure of a surprise. A door opens at the top of a flight of steps; down come a well-groomed man and young boy—Muslims with small round hats. They invite the strangers into their home to see the family mosque. So politely, gracefully given, the invitation is accepted. It is a wonderful room, walled with lustrous blue-and-white Chinese tiles, possibly Ming. The ceiling is covered with gilt-framed mirrors reflecting the sparkle of several crystal chandeliers. The west wall, the Mecca wall, is mirrored. There, on a low golden mantle, the Holy Koran rests in a gold, filigree box. Heaped around it, fresh flowers are punctuated with crystal perfume bottles, their tall stoppers like exclamation marks of devotion. The host opens a mirror-masked door, whirls a safe-knob and brings out a bottle of rare scent, a ruby-colored essence distilled from an Oriental bouquet. A drop

Inside an old house in Delhi; chess has been a favorite pastime for centuries

on each hand envelops the adventurers in a cloud of heady perfume as they walk down to the square.

Three young men with Hindu prayer-marks on their foreheads wait with still another invitation. A famous *sadhu*—Hindu holy man—from a well-known and ancient retreat high in the Himalayas, is visiting them. Inside in the shadows of a marble colonnade, clusters of women sit on the floor, their fine white-cotton saris—the saris worn for prayer—are pulled across their bowed heads. In the deepest shadow, beside the three glowing crossed sticks of a little sacred fire, sits the young *sadhu*. His skin is gray with ashes. Sandalwood beads, a three-cord sacred thread, and a hip-wrapping cotton cloth are his clothes. The sacred ashes of humility also powder his long hair. He has vermillion marks on his forehead and a benign light on his face. While he stays, the house will be crowded day and night with devotees from many parts of the city who come to hear him teach from the Vedas, the ancient Hindu scriptures. After a few weeks he will go to another house. A number of pears lie near him, rare delicacies brought as an offering. As they leave, the priest solemnly gives a pear to each of the foreign visitors.

The next quiet passage ends in the chaos of the jewelry bazaar. Rickshaws careen, bicycle bells clang, beggars whine, handcart pullers shout, everyone pushes. You must shoulder your way through. Then a conniving voice speaks close to your ears: "Emeralds? Rubies? Come with me!" An old, turbaned fellow is measuring you and your companions with practiced eyes. Saying "Why not?" you follow him. Dodging, twisting along a hectic side street and into a shabby doorway, you fumble down a dim passage to a steep dark staircase, and climb after the nimble old man.

Rough doors, chopped into the stairwell, open on makeshift platforms slung just below the ceiling of once-lofty doors, and divided into tiny cubicles. People darting in and out of these improvised homes testify to the cruel pressures of poverty. The bazaar roar drums through the building. There are eddies of curry-scented air. Another turn and you step out onto a roof. Sun pours down; a trellis supports a burden of vines.

As you stop to catch your breath the old man jumps between you and an enormous Alsatian that has leaped round the trellis. The jeweler's watchdog is well trained: a word from the tall man who skirts the green barricade to welcome you, and the monster wags off on his vigilant round. Behind the trellis, under a vine-covered canopy, men are sorting gems, writing, or calculating. You and your friends sit on a long white cushion. Cold Cola drinks appear, bottles open and invitingly sprouting straws. Papers of unset stones are spread out—a fistful of pale sapphires, a dazzling sugarbowl full of tiny diamonds. There are topazes carved into autumn leaves, emerald leaves green as spring, roses of rubies, a pale emerald lotus —ample treasure for the dog to guard.

Old Delhi roofs are put to many uses. At certain seasons an insistent, high-pitched but delicate whistle pierces the sunny sky. On a different key, from a different direction, comes another whistle. Then in wheeling arcs, silvery-winged pigeons whirl up, ribbon out through the

Kite flyers take over the roofs in early autumn

air and flutter down to their home roofs again. Pigeon flying was a favorite Mogul pastime, and no gentle sport. The hereditary pigeoner trained his birds in intricate flight patterns and for races where large sums were bet. His whistle controlled every movement of well-trained birds and excitement mounted when, by clever whistling, he steered his flock near a rival's. In the confusion—and this is still part of the fun today, though the sport is much less exacting now—irresolute birds were enticed away by the firm allegiance of the well trained who sometimes led a whole rival flock to the winner's roof.

Kite flyers take over the roofs during early autumn. On a certain day in September, called the Birthday of Paper Kites, roofs are crowded. The blue, cloud-heaped, post-monsoon sky dances with a clever confetti of bright-colored, diamond-shaped paper kites. The Moguls thought of gluing ground glass to the kite string, and thus developed kite-fighting to a fine art, still popular today in spite of generations of cut fingers. Money is sometimes tied to kites. Then the bettors shout an equivalent of "Come on, Purple," "Come on, Red," as the kites swing into battle high in the sky. The expert will manage to entangle a rival's kite, sever the string by adroitly manipulated, glass-sharpened jerks, and bring down the trophy. On Kite Birthday Evening, box kites, carrying lighted candles, are cut adrift and sail mysteriously into the calm night—brief, glowing reminders of a fantastic and receding age.

In winter, a sunny roof is a pleasant place for household chores. The women of the house gather with their flat, stone mortars and stone pestles to chat and gossip while they grind spices for the day's curry.

In the very heart of the Old Delhi bazaars is a surprising knoll. Small houses line the steep lane that winds up Water Tank Hill. After a short climb on the rough cobbles, the traffic and the turmoil vanish. The only sounds are of children playing in the lane, of old men chatting in the shade of a wall. A bell-ringing bicycle careens down. Its noise will add to the market furor; here it is a pleasant streak of carefree sound. At the top, the walls stop against a big pillar-perched water tank. Little huts and houses have sprouted on the slope as if they, too, are nourished by the reservoir's generous leaks that have greened the crest with wild grass. Below, spreads Old

Delhi's jumble of flat roofs crazily stacked, a town of play-blocks tumbled by a giant child. Shapely domes and minarets—that look so excitingly Oriental from the air when the travelers' planes arrive—ornament the scene. Jama Masjid and many others, each with its own rich history, wait to be discovered.

This whole area—shabby, congested, and intriguing— was a center of fury during the bitter days of the Mutiny (in 1857, North India was swept by an abortive rebellion against British rule, which resulted in the firm establishment of British sovereignty over India).

The Old City tumult ends on the north at Kashmiri Gate and a bit of old, gray-stone City Wall, both deeply scarred by Mutiny cannon fire. Just inside the Gate, white-columned St. James's Church stands in a lovely garden, the fulfilled promise of a flamboyant Englishman,

Kashmiri Gate, the north end of Old Delhi, leads to the Civil Lines

St. James's Church

Colonel James Skinner, famous cavalry commander of Skinner's Horse. Seriously wounded in the Mutiny, Skinner vowed to build a church if he recovered. He not only built St. James's, but a Muslim mosque and a Hindu temple as well. Near the church, several old-fashioned shops, famous for luxury goods in British-India days, are still possible treasure troves.

Beyond Kashmiri Gate, in the Civil Lines of Old Delhi, there are two inviting Mogul Gardens, Roshanara and Qudsia, romantic places for an afternoon's stroll. Trees are great with age, vines cover tumbling gatehouse walls and fallen mosques. A number of big hotels have survived the shift of business to New Delhi, attracting guests all the way to Civil Lines by their beautiful garden settings.

The University, however, is the real magnet today

for this sedate part of the city. Lively students fill buses and street cars. Girl students, hair in braids, cluster in laughing, soft-voiced groups. On every avenue, vital young India's twinkling bicycle brigade sweeps toward the campus to learn about the expanding horizons of our modern world.

When classes are over, students love to stroll on the Ridge that thrusts along the University's south boundary. There is a motor road, but they prefer the paths winding through a wild growth of yellow-flowered jungle acacia trees and red-blossomed smoke-ash. From the observatory room of the Mutiny Memorial they see old Flagstaff Tower. Looking north, they watch the Ashoka Pillar of

Girl students cluster in laughing, soft-voiced groups on the campus at Delhi University

the Ridge gather another evening to itself. Dusk veils two scars on this ancient symbol of peace, wounds of Mutiny cannon fire that broke it into three parts. The lights of evening are soon visible.

Year after year, the observant student will see more lights and richer patterns as the vigorous New-Old city extends her borders.

The Mutiny Memorial

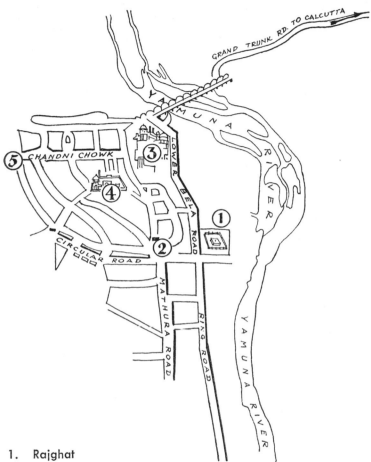

1. Rajghat
2. Delhi Gate
3. Red Fort
4. Jama Masjid
5. Fatehpur Mosque

FROM RAJGHAT TO FATEHPUR MOSQUE

FROM CENTRAL VISTA TO PURANA QILA, SOUTH TO

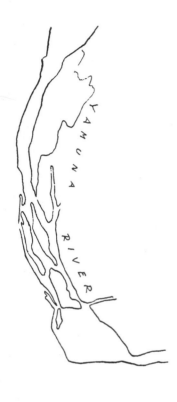

1. Connaught Place
2. Secretariats
3. President's house
4. Indian Gardens (Mughul)
5. India Gate and Prince's Park
6. Prime Minister's house
7. Parliament House
8. Church of Redemption
9. National Museum
10. National Archives
11. Jaipur House
12. Supreme Court
13. National Stadium
14. Purana Qila
15. Zoo
16. Sundar Nagar
17. Friend's Colony
18. Golf Links
19. Jor Bagh
20. Tomb of Nizam-ud-Din
21. Lodi Gardens
22. Humayun's tomb
23. Safdar-Jung's tomb
24. Safdarjung Airport
25. Race Course

FRIEND'S COLONY, AND WEST TO RACE COURSE

FROM DIPLOMATIC ENCLAVE

TO WILLINGDON CRESCENT, EAST TO

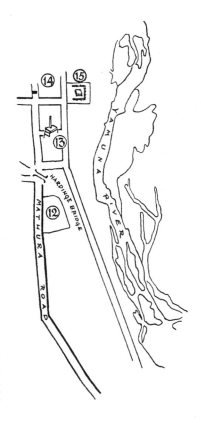

1. Diplomatic Enclave
2. Hotel Ashoka
3. Capitol Buildings
4. National Laboratory
5. Agricultural Research Institute
6. New Hindu Temple
7. Talkatora Gardens
8. Cathedral of the Sacred Heart
9. All India Radio Building
10. Jantar Mantar
11. Central Post Office
12. Exhibition Grounds
13. Kotla
14. Delhi Gate
15. Rajghat

AGRICULTURAL RESEARCH INSTITUTE

AND WEST TO RAJGHAT

131

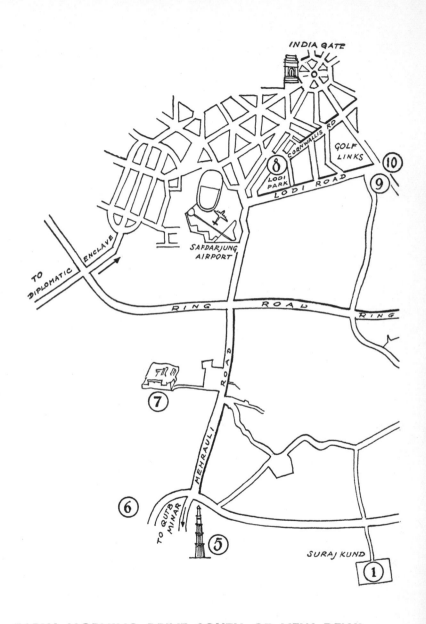

EARLY MORNING DRIVE SOUTH OF NEW DELHI

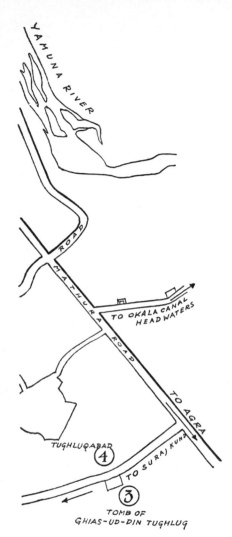

1. Suraj Kund
2. Anangpala's Dam
3. Tomb of Ghias-ud-Din Tughlug
4. Tughluqabad
5. Qutb Minar (in enclosure:
   Iltamish tomb, House of Balban,
   Alai Darwaza, Alai Minar,
   Ghori Durgah)
6. Mehrauli Village
7. Hauz-Khas and Firoz Shah's tomb
8. Lodi Tomb
9. Tomb of Nizam-ud-Din
10. Humayun's Tomb

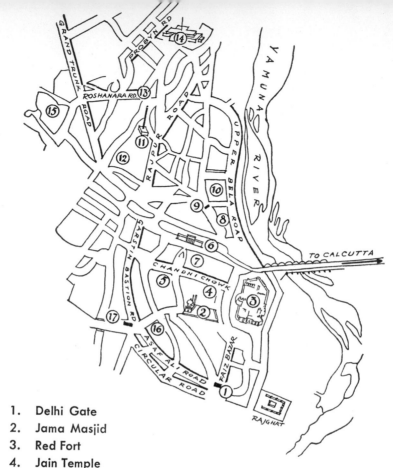

1. Delhi Gate
2. Jama Masjid
3. Red Fort
4. Jain Temple
5. Sikh Gurdwara
6. Railway Station
7. Library
8. St. James Church
9. Kashmiri Gate
10. Qudsia Gardens
11. Ashoka Ridge Column (Iron Pillar)
12. Mutiny Memorial
13. Flagstaff Tower
14. Delhi University
15. Roshanara Gardens
16. Water Tank Hill
17. Ajmeri Gate

OLD DELHI: FROM DELHI GATE TO MUTINY MEMORIAL

INDEX

135

139

homes in, 14, 117–119; as capital of Mogul Dynasty, 14; shops and bazaars in, 14, 17, 18; occupations and customs of people in, 14–18; description of, 14–21; streets in, 15, 16, 18, 21, 23, *see also names of;* public buildings of, 15, 21; earlier times in, 16; mills in, 16–17; crafts in, 17; fruit sellers in, 18; food and restaurants in, 18–19; work hours in, 24–25; government of, 29; population of, 30; Gandhi's shrine near, 32; grave of Reziya in, 50; Spring festival in, 54; Tibetan traders in bazaars of, 94; streets leading to, 99, 101; uses of roofs of, 120–122; from Water Tank Hill, 122; north end of, 123; *see also* Delhi *and* New Delhi

Old Fort, *see* Purana Qila

Orissa, 86

paan man, 18

Pakistan, 31, 68

Palace of Color, 112

Palam, International Airport, 9, 63

Palam Airport Highway, 89

Pali Script, 102

Panchsheel Marg, 89

Pandavas, 34

parks and gardens, 26–28; National, at Purana Qila, 76; at Red Fort, 108–109; near Red Fort and Friday Mosque, 116; in Civil Lines, 124; *see also names of*

Parliament, Upper and Lower Houses of, 68

Parliament House, 68

Parliament Street, 14, 65, 93

Peacock Throne, 111, 112

Pearl Mosque, at Red Fort, 109

people, occupations of, in Old Delhi, 14, 16–18; customs and pleasures of, 15, 25–26, 27–28, 81; Western, in New Delhi, 80–81; helpfulness of, 99; and Gandhi, 104; *see also* youth *and* family life

Persians, conquering of Delhi by 36, 76, 78, 79, 107, 111–112; couplet of, on arch in Diwan-i-Khas, 110

pigeon-flying, 120–121

pillar, iron, *see* Iron Pillar

pillars, Ashokan, *see* Ashokan Columns

Pillar Edicts of Ashoka, 102

policemen, description of, 30

polo, 84, 86

population, 14, 30, 31

President, 66–67, 72–73; *see also* President's House

President's House, 13–14, 65–66; visitors' tours of, 67

Prime Minister, 67, 68, 86, 113

Prince's Park, 71

Princep, James, 102

Prithviraj Chauhan, 43–44

public buildings, *see* buildings, public

Punjab, 36, 51, 53, 115–116

Purana Qila, 28, 72; outer bastion and gates of, 76; and Humayun, 76, 78; seventh city of Delhi, 78–79; village under walls of, 80

143

Timur, 62, 78

tombs, in parks and gardens, 27–28, 82; oldest, in India, 50; *see also names of specific tombs*

traffic, 11; in Connaught Place, 12; at rush hours, 12, 24; focal points of, 65; at Diplomatic Enclave, 88

transportation, 23–24, 88; *see also* traffic

travel agencies, 99

trees, in New Delhi, 26–27, 89

"Truth Alone Triumphs," 87

Tughluq Dynasty, 57, 59

Tughluqabad, 57, 59

tulsi bush, 80

Turks, invasion of Rai Pithora by, 43–44; murder of Queen Reziya by, 50; nature of sultans of, 60

Udaipur, polo in, 84

Vaisyas, duties of, 35

Vedas, 119

Vindhya Hills, trains through, to Delhi, 10

War Memorial Arch, *see* India Gate

Water Tank Hill, 122

weather, *see* temperature *and* monsoons

Wheel of Order, 68

Willingdon Crescent, 89

winter, season for tourists in Delhi, 10; sports events in, 84; roofs used in, 122

Women's Pavilion, *see* Rang Mahal

work, hours of, 24–25; *see also* occupations

Yamuna River, 32; air view of, 9; as guardian of India, 33, 36, 40; and Aryans, 35; part played by, in life of city, 37, 40; flooding of, 37–38; cremation terraces on banks of, 38–39; factories on banks of, 39; view of, from Raisina Hill, 64; seen from Hotel Ashoka, 88; Firozabad at edge of, 102

youth, way of life of, 15, 22–23; festivals for, 53–54; and Rama plays, 100; *see also* people *and* family life

Zoo, *see* New Delhi Zoo

Printed in U.S.A.